S0-BBF-455

NEW LIFE
in
CHRIST

NEW LIFE

in

CHRIST

WHAT REALLY HAPPENS
WHEN YOU'RE BORN AGAIN AND
WHY IT MATTERS

STEVEN J. LAWSON

BakerBooks

a division of Baker Publishing Group
Grand Rapids, Michigan

© 2020 by Steven J. Lawson

Published by Baker Books
a division of Baker Publishing Group
PO Box 6287, Grand Rapids, MI 49516-6287
www.bakerbooks.com

Printed in the United States of America

All rights reserved. No part of this publication may be reproduced, stored in a retrieval system, or transmitted in any form or by any means—for example, electronic, photocopy, recording—without the prior written permission of the publisher. The only exception is brief quotations in printed reviews.

Library of Congress Cataloging-in-Publication Data
Names: Lawson, Steven J., author.
Title: New life in Christ : what really happens when you're born again and why it matters / Steven J. Lawson.
Description: Grand Rapids : Baker Books, a division of Baker Publishing Group, 2020.
Identifiers: LCCN 2019027436 | ISBN 9780801094859 (paperback)
Subjects: LCSH: Salvation—Christianity.
Classification: LCC BT751.3 .L39 2020 | DDC 234—dc23
LC record available at https://lccn.loc.gov/2019027436

Scripture quotations are from the New American Standard Bible® (NASB), copyright © 1960, 1962, 1963, 1968, 1971, 1972, 1973, 1975, 1977, 1995 by The Lockman Foundation. Used by permission. www.Lockman.org

Some names and details have been changed to protect the privacy of the individuals involved.

20 21 22 23 24 25 26   7 6 5 4 3 2 1

In keeping with biblical principles of creation stewardship, Baker Publishing Group advocates the responsible use of our natural resources. As a member of the Green Press Initiative, our company uses recycled paper when possible. The text paper of this book is composed in part of post-consumer waste.

This book is dedicated to

Richard and Bobbie Grogan

Your loyal and trusted friendship has been a constant source
of encouragement to me for the past twenty-five years.

Contents

Foreword

Sometimes a brief conversation can change the whole course of your life. It may begin casually with a nod or a smile to someone you sit down beside, and two years later (or even earlier) you are working for them—or are even married to them—or perhaps you simply receive new light on your situation that changes your whole perspective on things.

For the rest of your life, you look back on that conversation and realize it was a game changer. Even if it began in the same way a thousand conversations did, with a few polite words, by its end you know that your life may never be the same again.

Dr. Steven Lawson's book *New Life in Christ* could prove to be just such a conversation partner in your life. I hope it will.

Sometimes reading a book can feel like having a conversation with its author. You, the reader, are listening to what the author is saying—and you are responding, talking back to him or her, even if it is silently. You may be saying, "That's interesting," or "Really, tell me more," or even "I don't see that; explain it to me."

You may well find yourself having a conversation just like that as you read these pages. But what you are about to discover is that, intriguingly, this book contains not one but two conversations!

The first is a conversation Steve Lawson wants to have with you. He is eager to talk to you—and, in fact, he has plenty to say, so expect him to do most of the talking (and if you have ever heard him speak you will probably be able to hear his voice as you read). In *New Life in Christ*, Steve has a very direct conversational style. He is talking to *you*—so much so that perhaps you will find yourself talking back to him, at least inwardly!

But then, after a few pages, this first conversation is mainly about another conversation—one of the most important in all human history, and one that gives us perhaps the best-known words in the New Testament.

This conversation is between Jesus and Nicodemus, a contemporary of Jesus and a man of great distinction in Jerusalem. He was a Pharisee, a member of the Jewish Ruling Council, the Sanhedrin, and—according to Jesus Himself—the great theologian of his day in Israel. Interestingly, it was Nicodemus who sought out Jesus, not the other way around. But we never learn exactly why. And soon he found that Jesus was seeking him. Fascinating!

So, you are about to overhear a historic conversation. And in the background Steve Lawson, like a knowledgeable commentator at some major event, will help you to understand what is going on and will discuss the different "moves" the two men make in the chess-like conversation they have with each other.

It is time to make yourself comfortable, turn the page, and read the first chapter. And in your mind's eye, see Nicodemus making his way under the darkening night sky, his robes blowing around him as the evening wind begins to freshen, and arriving at the house where Jesus is. The two men are about to meet. How long their conversation stretched out we don't know. What we do know is that Nicodemus never forgot it. Nor will you.

But now, like a TV continuity announcer, I have filled my three-minute slot; the real dialogue will soon begin. For further conversation, I am glad to leave you in the reliable hands of your expert commentator Steve Lawson. You are in for a significant hour or two in his company!

Sinclair B. Ferguson
Chancellor's Professor, Reformed Theological Seminary
Teaching Fellow, Ligonier Ministries

one

Born Again

But as many as received Him, to them He gave the right to become children of God, even to those who believe in His name, who were born, not of blood nor of the will of the flesh nor of the will of man, but of God.

JOHN 1:12–13

On a dark Colorado night, beneath towering, majestic mountains, a young teenage boy walked between the pine trees to be alone with God. He had just heard a message from the Bible recounting when Jesus turned water into wine. This divine miracle that occurred two thousand years ago revealed how an embarrassed family ran out of wine at their wedding feast. When Jesus's mother appealed to Him to intervene, He told the assistants to fill six empty water pots with water.

When the pots were brought to Jesus, He did what only He can do. Jesus transformed the dirty, stagnant water into pure, sparkling wine. When the wine was presented to the headwaiter, he was shocked. Every other wedding party, he explained, serves the best wine first. Then, after the people have drunk freely, they bring out the poorer wine. But this wedding did the inexplicable. It saved the best for last.

The speaker said, "This is what Jesus must do in your life. He must take your dirty, dingy, stagnant life, polluted by sin, and transform it into the purest and best a person could ever experience."

He added, "This miracle by Jesus is a picture of the new birth that must take place in your life. This is what Jesus must do within you. You must be born again."

At the conclusion of the message, the speaker had asked each person not to talk to anyone but to go out into the cool summer night and search their heart. He asked, "Where are you with God? Has He ever changed you from the inside out? If this has never happened to you, ask God to cause you to be born again. Commit your life to Jesus Christ."

A Heart-Searching Time

Walking out into the quietness of the night, the teenage boy grappled with these gospel truths. He looked into his heart, thinking, *Where am I with God? How can I have this new start with God?* He desired to have this new heart the speaker spoke of. He looked up into the sky above and put his trust in Jesus Christ.

In that moment, a miracle occurred within him. The soiled water became sparkling wine. His life was changed. He was born again.

This transformation was a miracle of grace. It was a work performed by God so His glory would be put on display. I know

14

this account is true. I know that teenage boy was changed. I know his dirty heart was transformed into the best it could be.

I know, because I was that teenage boy.

The Miracle of the New Birth

What comes into your mind when you hear the phrase "born again"? What is the new birth? What is the nature of being born again? And why is such a new start in life so necessary?

These are important questions that require our careful answers. Few truths need clear teaching more than the new birth. Because of muddled teaching, few doctrines are less understood by believers—and even much less understood by unbelievers. Yet no truth is more important in order to understand what God does when someone enters His kingdom. Rather than just a slight shift in the heart, rebirth is a complete spiritual overhaul of the soul. Instead of a mere addition to someone's life, rebirth means a person possesses an entirely new life.

The new birth is not like repainting an old house, going over an old layer of paint. Rather, it completely tears down the house and builds an entirely new structure on the same site. Such a person becomes a whole new creation. The old life is taken down and a new life is built in its place.

Being born again means that God implants divine life within our spiritually dead heart. It is the life-giving act of God, whereby He causes us to be birthed into His family. It means that by the supernatural work of the Holy Spirit, we are dramatically transformed in the core of our being. When we are born anew, we are made alive to God. In the new birth, God gives us new life that only He can give.

Grasping the New Birth

In order to better grasp what the new birth is, I want us to begin by considering the first passage in the Bible that actually records the words "born of God." It is found in the opening chapter of the Gospel of John.

> But as many as received Him, to them He gave the right to become children of God, even to those who believe in His name, who were born, not of blood nor of the will of the flesh nor of the will of man, but of God. (John 1:12–13)

In these verses, we are first introduced to the analogy of being born of God. However, this is not the earliest mention in Scripture of this spiritual reality. Throughout the Old Testament the new birth is represented by other metaphors such as a heart circumcision (Deut. 30:6), a heart transplant (Ezek. 36:25–27), and a spiritual resurrection (Ezek. 37:1–10). Nevertheless, John 1:13 is the first mention of the new birth. Many other passages in the New Testament also use this metaphor of birth (John 3:3, 5–6; 1 John 3:9; 5:1, 4–5, 18).

All Things New

In this opening section, the apostle John mentions this divine work of grace that gives new spiritual life. This describes what takes place when anyone enters into the kingdom of God. This new birth enables a person to become a believer in Jesus as Lord and Savior. It gives a new beginning with God, the new start that everyone needs. This divine intervention is the radical and complete transformation of a person's life that is performed by God.

The new birth gives the life of God—*divine* life, *eternal* life, *supernatural* life—to a previously empty, lifeless soul. Where once there was only a hollow existence, divine life was created in the soul—*real* life, *new* life, *abundant* life. For the first time, a person begins to live as God intended him or her to live. Jesus said, "I came that they may have life, and have it abundantly" (John 10:10). This new birth gives personal knowledge of God by creating spiritual life within the heart. The accompanying changes include a new desire for God and a passion for His word. Simply put, being born of God is divine life within the soul.

Remarkably, there are two sides of this one entrance into the kingdom of God. On one side is the person's activity. The other side involves God's activity. In John 1:12, John describes the step of faith required to become a child of God. The apostle John begins with the human responsibility to believe in Christ. In verse 13, he then tells us it is God who causes individuals to be born again. Both aspects are necessary. We must understand what part each plays in order to have a proper understanding of these essential truths.

From the Human Side

The apostle John begins verse 12 with the word *but*. This marks a sharp contrast with what preceded in the immediate context. Earlier, John noted that Jesus Christ "was in the world, and the world was made through Him, and the world did not know Him" (1:10). Jesus was the Creator of the world, *but* the world He made did not recognize Him when He appeared. The splendor of His eternal deity was veiled by the sinless human nature and flesh that He took on. He did not enter this world with the

17

pomp and majesty of a ruling sovereign. Instead, He came in the form of a lowly servant. He was truly God, yet His royalty was concealed in a human body. He set aside the radiant display of His glory for the rags of humble humanity. Consequently, the unbelieving eyes of humankind did not recognize Him for who He truly was.

John further explains, "He came to His own, and those who were His own did not receive Him" (v. 11). How strange that the very world Jesus created did not receive Him. This is because the spiritual eyes of the people were blinded by their own sin. They could not recognize Him as their Creator and Savior. Neither could they ascertain that He was their long-awaited Messiah. For the most part, His sovereign claims fell upon spiritually deaf ears.

Receiving Jesus Christ

However, there was a remnant who did believe in Jesus Christ. John explains that "as many as received Him, to them He gave the right to become children of God" (v. 12). Those who "received" Him welcomed Him into their lives as a host would warmly receive a guest. This glad reception meant the beginning of a close, intimate relationship with Him. Christ comes to live in the ones who believe in Him. This divinely bestowed right as "children" includes addressing God as Father and becoming a joint heir with Christ, sharing in the vast estate bequeathed by the Father to His Son. This right entitles those who receive Jesus as Lord and Savior to His vast inheritance. This privilege includes receiving God's abundant provision for daily needs and His continual protection. It also means one day in the future abiding in the Father's house in heaven above.

Believing in His Name

John further identifies those who receive Jesus Christ as "those who believe in His name" (v. 12). In other words, receiving Christ is the same as believing in Him. To "believe" in Jesus means more than merely knowing some intellectual facts about Him or simply acknowledging who He is and what He came to do. To believe in Him includes far more than feeling emotions about Jesus, being deeply convicted of your sin, and even being persuaded of your desperate need for Him. Believing in Jesus means more than recognizing He is the only One who can deliver you from your sin problem.

To believe in Jesus Christ is a decisive act of the will by which a person commits his or her life to Him. Believing in Jesus means entrusting our life to Him in humble submission. It involves surrendering our life to Him as our Lord and submitting to His supreme authority. It necessitates denying ourselves and following Him. Anyone who becomes a child of God does so by believing in Jesus Christ.

Why Did You Believe?

But an important question needs to be raised. *Why* do some believe in Jesus Christ while others do not? Why do some receive Him into their life but others refuse Him? Why do some have a relationship with Him yet others do not know Him? Is it because those who believe are smarter? Is it because they are better people? Were they more spiritual?

The answers to these questions are found in the next verse, as John records, "[They] were born, not of blood nor of the will of the flesh nor of the will of man, but of God" (1:13). Having considered the human responsibility to receive Jesus, the apostle John next describes the divine work in the new birth. God must cause a person to be born again, which, in turn, produces saving faith. It is the new birth that enables us to receive Jesus Christ into our life. The decisive factor in anyone coming to faith in Christ, John explains, is that they are "born . . . of God" (v. 13). This refers not to our physical birth but to our spiritual birth.

This new birth is like the creation of the new heaven and new earth, when all things will be made new. Though we still retain elements of our old life, our whole being is changed instantaneously and dramatically into a brand-new, God-glorifying life.

New Life from God

Being born of God means that new life is created by Him within a human heart. This is the conceiving of the life of God Himself within a spiritually dead soul. Before the new birth, Paul writes, "You were dead in your trespasses and sins" (Eph. 2:1). That is, each unbeliever is a living corpse, devoid of any spiritual life. We are walking dead in this world. But when we are reborn, God breathes new life into the empty vacuum of our human soul. This divine act raises us from the grave of sin to eternal life.

The new birth brings an entirely new quality of life that only God can give. It is entirely unlike anything this world can give—an out-of-this-world life that comes down from God above. Regeneration sparks a supernatural life unlike anything we previously experienced. When we are born again, the previously defiled soul is cleansed from the stains of sin. Our old heart of stone, once hardened toward God, is removed. In its place, a new heart of flesh is implanted within our inner person. This gives our heart a spiritual pulse that is alive to God.

The Holy Spirit assumes His royal residence within our innermost being. Our heart comes alive to God, and it immediately responds to Him. The Spirit causes us to start to walk in the path of righteousness. This rebirth produces a radical change of life. The old things have passed away, and our souls have been washed clean. Our new heart is made free from the dominating power of sin, and we have a new desire to pursue the things of God.

Negatives and Positive

The apostle John explains more specifically how this new birth occurs. He uses three negative denials followed by one positive assertion to make his point. He first states how the second birth does *not* occur, then affirms how it *does* come to pass. By addressing this from both the negative and the positive, he leaves no room for misunderstandings. It may be difficult to accept this exclusive means to enter the kingdom of heaven, but that message is crystal clear.

By stating this from both sides of the truth, John explains in simple terms how the new birth comes to pass. Regeneration is not a cooperative effort between two parties or a joint project involving two equals. Instead, the new birth is exclusively a divine work of God in the human heart.

Not by Our Family Heritage

John's first negative denial explains that those who enter the kingdom of God "were born, not of blood" (1:13). No one is birthed into the family of God because of their family heritage. We are not made right with God simply because we are born into a Christian family or with Jewish blood. Our family lineage does not create new life within us. Our physical descent does not automatically act as a catalyst for our spiritual birth.

We may be born into a Christian family but that does not make us a member of God's family. God has many children but no grandchildren. Our parent may have been an elder or deacon in the church in which we grew up. Our grandparent may have been a missionary to a remote part of the earth. Our great-grandparent may have been a pastor. We may be a seventh-generation descendant of a famous figure in church history. But this religious pedigree cannot birth anyone into God's family.

Not by Our Personal Efforts

Further, John stipulates that the new birth is not "of the will of the flesh" (v. 13). This means that being born again is not the result of any moral efforts. It does not come from going to church, knowing Scripture, or even reciting a prayer. In other words, the new birth is not produced by the good works that a person has performed. No involvement in any religious routine or church attendance can gain someone entrance into the kingdom of God.

By way of analogy, there was nothing any of us could do to cause our physical birth. We did not have any moral ability to cause it. What could we possibly have done to cause our birth? The answer, of course, is nothing. In like manner, there is nothing anyone can do to produce their spiritual birth into the family of God. There is no contribution we could possibly make to cause our own spiritual conception. We are utterly powerless to create eternal life within ourselves.

Not by Our Personal Choice

Moreover, John is emphatic that the new birth was not caused by "the will of man" (v. 13). This denies that any personal choice a person would make could result in him or her being born again. The exercise of the will by an unconverted person to believe in Jesus Christ is entirely impossible. After all, what can a dead person do? The answer is absolutely nothing. None of us has the capacity to choose to be born. Neither do we have the ability to choose to be born again.

When anyone believes in Jesus Christ, it is with saving faith that did not originate with them. Dead people cannot believe. God must first originate new life within each dead heart. He must create saving faith. Only then are we enabled to respond to the gospel. It is God who must turn our unbelieving heart toward Christ. We, the dead, must recognize our complete inability to save ourselves and cry out to God for salvation. Even the repentance by which a person turns away from sin is the gift of God. The exercise of the will is never the cause of the new birth but the result of it. Every aspect of conversion is traced directly back to God in the new birth.

But by God's Working

The apostle John then advances beyond the three negative denials to one positive assertion. He concludes that being born from above is "of God" (v. 13). This is to say, the new birth takes place entirely by God's working in our soul. Regeneration is exclusively the saving activity of God. What a person cannot do, God must do—and does do. In the new birth, He creates new life where none previously existed. God must cause a spiritual conception within the barren womb of our heart.[He then must induce labor and bring about the delivery of new life.]

From this divine perspective, it is clear that the ultimate reason anyone believes in Jesus Christ is because we are born again. The new birth gives new eyes to see the truth of the gospel. It gives new ears to hear what God is saying in His word. It gives a new heart to love God with a new affection. It gives new feet to come to Christ by faith. It gives new hands to embrace Him.

A Brand-New You

This is the greatest miracle God ever performs. Every other display of divine power is a distant second to His causing the new birth. We who are born again are never the same again. We are a new creation by the undeserved grace of God. The new birth begins the divine work of remaking each person into the likeness of Jesus Christ.

In the chapters that follow, we will examine the personal encounter that one man had with Jesus Christ, recorded in John 3. He was a noted individual who lived two thousand years ago, during the time of the Lord's public ministry. We will examine the nighttime rendezvous between this highly revered religious leader, Nicodemus, and the one he approached, Jesus Christ. As we investigate this meeting, we will discover more clearly what God does in our life when He causes us to be born again. To rightly appreciate His saving power, we must know more about this miracle of the new birth.

Before you turn the page, I must ask you: Have you experienced this new birth? If so, this book will clarify what God has already done in your life. If you have not been born again, please continue reading, because the following pages will explain more carefully what God must do in your life. In reality, you must become a miracle of grace.

two

Elusive Search

Now there was a man of the Pharisees, named Nicodemus,
a ruler of the Jews.

JOHN 3:1

Before I was born again, I looked for fulfillment in many things. As a young man, I lived for sports. I played football, basketball, and baseball year-round. Athletics was where I found my greatest excitement, temporal as it was. I loved the thrill of competition and the sense of accomplishment. I pursued everything that came with athletics, including the applause and affirmation.

It may have been different for you. Before you were born again, you may have sought happiness in other things. It may have been grades or music. It may have been friends or travel—or an exhilarating experience. Whatever it was, you were ever searching until you found God—or rather until God found you.

The Pursuit

Everyone searches for what they believe will bring them happiness. We look far and wide for this elusive something that we perceive will give us fulfillment. What this is, we do not know. We just know that something is missing. We keep looking, ever searching, but never finding it in the things of this world.

Relationships and Career

Perhaps we try to fill this vacuum with a meaningful relationship. Maybe we meet someone special. We fall in love. We get married. We expect that this new person will fill the void within, and this new companionship initially satisfies this longing. But inevitably, the relationship becomes strained. Expectations are unmet. Feelings are hurt. What we yearn for is not found there. We have to look elsewhere.

Maybe we try to fill this emptiness with a promising career. We may find initial significance in a new job. We may attempt to satisfy our inner hunger by moving up the corporate ladder. We try earning a better living. But we soon realize that our new position requires longer hours. This new responsibility means working under a demanding boss. We may be treated unfairly. We are passed over for a sought-after promotion. We soon become more frustrated than before we started this new position. This job did not deliver what we thought. We remain restless and unsatisfied. We have to look someplace else for what is missing.

Possessions and Religion

We may think what we lack can be found in money and possessions. We may think that if we could have more money in our bank account, we would be happy. If we could somehow purchase a larger house and live in a better neighborhood, we would be satisfied. If we could afford to send our children to better schools, then we would be fulfilled. But we come to the sobering realization that what we yearn for is not found in possessions. We have to look in another direction.

Maybe we look to fill this inner void by crowding our calendar with religious activities. We may start attending a church. Perhaps we join a Bible study. Maybe we volunteer for a community charity. We initially feel better about ourselves. Our conscience is momentarily salved. But then the group dynamics change. The leader shows him- or herself to be a hypocrite. One of the members comes across as two-faced. A division erupts. Any true fulfillment is definitely not found here. So we keep searching.

Addictions and Self-Worth

Perhaps we try to fill this emptiness with destructive addictions. Maybe we seek a high from drugs. Maybe we gamble heavily. We may have an extramarital affair. Maybe we break the law. Whatever it may be, we are always searching for the emotional buzz we think these things can offer. But the rush of adrenaline from living on the edge only provides a temporary fix. Such heart-pounding excitement inevitably leaves us with a feeling of shame in the morning. These momentary, fleeting pleasures lead us further away from true happiness and into deeper despair and restlessness.

Worst of all, we might look for fulfillment within ourselves. We may try to "find" ourselves or attempt to entertain ourselves. We think what we need is found by looking more in the mirror. We try to redefine ourselves with a new identity. We

29

repackage ourselves with a new look on social media. We adopt a new persona. But we soon discover that we are not the solution. Instead, we are the problem. The answer must lay outside of ourselves. But where can it be found?

None of these pursuits can fill the deepest longings of our soul or provide any true satisfaction that lasts. We are merely chasing after the wind and only grabbing a fistful of air. These quests over-promise but under-deliver. They only scratch the surface of our deepest desires. These alluring paths lead to nowhere meaningful and leave our true needs unmet.

The Most Unlikely Person

This futile pursuit for what is missing in life points to a most prominent man who lived two thousand years ago. At first glance, he was the least likely person who needed to be born again. This man was strictly religious and highly successful. He was outwardly moral and supremely regarded. He knew much *about* God. He had a head full of knowledge about Scripture and knew the Bible inside out, better than anyone else. He was a spiritual leader, revered by all who knew him. His name was Nicodemus.

But this prosperous individual knew *something* was missing. What that elusive something was, he did not know. This formative figure had everything going for him. He was well-connected at the loftiest tier of the political structure and had risen to the top of the religious hierarchy of the day. He was revered for his elevated stature and commanding influence. All classes in society looked up to him. He had all the spiritual answers to solve their problems—whether they were servants, lawyers, or other religious leaders. They looked to him to tell them about God. They came to him to interpret the Scriptures. They wanted him to tell them what the Bible meant. They listened to him explain how to live.

But Nicodemus had as many unanswered questions as anyone else—maybe even more. He had searched everywhere to find the answers. He looked to religion. He strived to live a righteous life. But he had not found anything that could satisfy his empty soul. This unfulfilling pursuit was gnawing at him. It was eating him alive.

Approaching Jesus

Where could Nicodemus turn to find the answers? He had heard about Jesus of Nazareth. Who had not? Everyone had heard about Him. Jesus was the talk of the country. Nicodemus had surely received reports about the profound teaching of this itinerate teacher. He had heard about the miracles He performed. He knew about the enormous crowds that followed Him everywhere. Given these credentials, Nicodemus *had* to meet Jesus.

But such an encounter would have to be a secret meeting. Nicodemus could not afford to be seen with Jesus. That would not look good for his sterling reputation. This backroom rendezvous would have to be under the cloak of night. In Nicodemus's frantic search for what was missing, he sought out this traveling preacher for any insight he might gain. He merely wanted Jesus to point him in the right direction. Maybe give him some new insight or share a few pointers. Maybe suggest to him some practical action steps.

Are you searching for answers? Are you exhausted from pursuing meaning in life? I would encourage you to look to the One who *is* the truth. Look to the only One who has the answers to what is missing in your life. That One is the Creator of life itself. I challenge you to hear what Jesus will say to Nicodemus, because it is exactly what He says to you.

Needing a New Life

It never entered Nicodemus's mind that he needed more than a new perspective on life. It never dawned on him that what he needed was a new life. This religious leader did not merely need one more activity to add to his already cluttered schedule. He did not need a new program to restructure his spiritual disciplines, a time management seminar, or a new routine for his personal life.

What Nicodemus needed was something entirely different. It would not come from this fallen world or from the realm of sterile religion. What this religious leader needed had to come from above and from a different realm—the eternal life only Jesus can give.

What he needed was to be born again.

Nicodemus never considered that he must start his life over. He never thought that he needed an entirely new beginning. He never considered that his supposedly impeccable life was what was wrong. All he knew was that he could not continue in the direction he was going. Something would have to change. Nicodemus was soon to learn what he so desperately needed to experience. He was about to hear the only answer that would fulfill his restless heart.

What Everyone Needs

What Nicodemus sought two millennia ago is precisely what we need today. Human nature has not changed. Our needs are the same. We do not need a few self-help instructions. We do not need to rearrange our behavior. We do not need a better life map for success or a new ladder to climb. Instead, what we need is the new life that only God can give. We need a life that is unlike anything this world can give, one radically different from whatever we have previously experienced. What we need is eternal life. And this new life comes exclusively through the new birth.

As we examine this one-on-one encounter Nicodemus had with Jesus, we discover the truth about our past. Before we were born again, we were not any different than this ancient religious leader. By being introduced to Nicodemus, we will learn much about our former life, if we are in Christ. What this man needed to discover so long ago is what we experience in our life through the new birth.

Remembering the Emptiness

Remember those past vain searches for fulfillment? Whether it was the pursuit to acquire things or the pursuit to achieve worldly success, it never delivered what it promised. Whether running after social prestige or attempting to reach a financial goal, we were seductively lured into these empty quests for happiness. But they were all dead-end pursuits. At one time or another, they may have brought fleeting gratification. But it quickly passed away. These temporal things could never fulfill our soul, which was made to be satisfied in the eternal God.

There is only one solution to our deepest yearnings. No matter where we are, or what we have done, the answer is always near us. The solution requires we look upward to God. He is the One who made us in His own image. He uniquely fashioned us to be like Him. We were created to know and adore

33

Him, to worship Him and give Him glory. If we are to find true satisfaction in life, it will only be found in a personal relationship with God. Only when we prize Him above all else will we find lasting joy.

Seeking God First

God prioritized Himself when He issued the first commandment as the most important one. It states, "You shall have no other gods before Me" (Exod. 20:3). This means God must take precedence in our life. No one must be more important to us than God. Nothing must compete with God for first place in our life. This was later stressed when Moses said, "You shall love the LORD your God with all your heart and with all your soul and with all your might" (Deut. 6:5).

From the very beginning of the Old Testament to the moment Nicodemus encountered Jesus—and on to this present moment—God has always stressed a religion of the heart. Even Old Testament rituals like circumcision were always meant to reflect a heart being set apart to God. The greatest commandment was given by Moses to the ancient people of Israel.

> Now, Israel, what does the LORD your God require from you, but to fear the LORD your God, to walk in all His ways and love Him, and to serve the LORD your God with all your heart and with all your soul, and to keep the LORD's commandments and His statutes which I am commanding you today for your good? (10:12–13)

Tragically, the Jews instead bypassed the heart and focused on external rule-keeping as the measure of their religion. Nevertheless, the Hebrew Scriptures showed, time and time again, God's desire for a new heart. Only a new heart can have supreme affection and foremost devotion for God.

Jesus Christ established this same priority when He said, "Seek first His kingdom and His righteousness, and all these things will be added to you" (Matt. 6:33). This is to say, we must desire God above all else. He must be number one in our soul. Our primary focus must be upon Him. We cannot become preoccupied with the mere trinkets of this world. We must make God our chief pursuit and greatest treasure and desire Him more than whatever benefits He can bestow. We must hunger for the eternal pleasures of the kingdom of God, not the vain pursuits of the kingdom of this world.

Where We Must Come

Once we come to know God, the gnawing emptiness within us is removed. In the new birth, the infinite Creator of the universe comes to live within each of us. The Giver of life floods our once-empty soul with the fullness of Himself. We are made a new creation with a new mindset. We are filled with new desires. We become entirely new beings at the deepest level and have new priorities with new passions. We begin to make new choices in a new direction, desiring to please God with every decision, whether small or large.

Sure, someone else who does not know God may look attractive to us. They may even appear successful. We might be tempted to trade places with them. But deep inside, they are restless and looking for what we have found. They may appear to have their life together. But that is a mere illusion. There is a bottomless void within them that can never be filled by

35

anything or anyone except God Himself. That is where we once lived—and once we find Christ, there is no going back.

New life begins with the new birth. This divine conception is a divine work in our innermost being, something that only God can do within us. This new life is the supernatural life of God Himself within our heart.

Changing the Real Self

The new birth is not merely rearranging the surface activities of our life. It is not just behavior modification. It is not simply restructuring our disciplines. Nor is it reshuffling our schedule. Being born again runs much deeper than this. The essence of our being is fundamentally changed at the deepest level. Being born from above radically alters us to the very core of our being. Instead of chasing after the allure of the world, our heart is now bent toward the worship of the glorious God.

When we experience the new birth, we no longer pursue the cheap imitations that this world offers. They promise much but deliver no lasting satisfaction. The life God intends us to live begins when we are born from above. Through the new birth, our vain striving for happiness ends. When we experience this new life, we find what we were missing and discover what we had been seeking.

Where Are You?

I pray that you have already been born again. If this is true, then you should rejoice and give thanks to God, who has given you this new life in Christ. As you keep reading, you will discover even greater reasons to give glory to God for your new birth.

You will realize even more about the wonder of what God has done for you in the new birth.

However, this work of God may not have occurred in your life yet. You may be realizing that you have never experienced this new life in Jesus Christ. If so, you are exactly where Nicodemus was. You have been misguided in your search for a relationship with God. If this is true for you, what you will read in these following pages will describe what has been missing in your life and help you understand what you need to receive from God.

May this new life from God become the reality within your soul. May your elusive search find its ultimate fulfillment in God Himself. If God gives this new heart to you, I can assure you that you will find everything for which your soul searches.

three

Hardest Prospect

Now there was a man of the Pharisees, named Nicodemus,
a ruler of the Jews.

JOHN 3:1

Who are the hardest people to reach with the gospel?
Who are the ones who appear the most difficult to
be converted to Jesus Christ? You might presume
that these individuals would include hard-core drug addicts or
those living an adulterous life. You might say the last person you
would expect to be born again is the person who never attends
church. Undoubtedly, all of these individuals present a serious
challenge to reach with the gospel.

However, the hardest people to reach with the gospel are
those who falsely presume they have a right relationship with
God. These individuals are often highly moral in their personal
life. Perhaps they are a notably respected religious leader or a

kind, merciful philanthropist. Perhaps they are an active servant in their church or community or give time in helping others. They may even give their financial resources to charitable causes. But having such a devout life blinds these people to their true need. They never see that they must be born again.

People who have a fine, upstanding status in religious circles most often assume the message of salvation is always for someone else. In their eyes, the gospel is for the abusive spouse and the delinquent parent. They suppose that the grace of God is for those who have committed a gross crime. True as this is, they never see that the gospel is for them. They assume nonreligious people are the only ones who need a new start with God. But they are oblivious to their own spiritual need.

This lack of self-awareness makes them the hardest people to reach with the gospel. They fail to understand that they need the new birth as much as anyone else. Their problem is not that they think they are too sinful to be saved. The very opposite is the case—they presume they are too good to need a new life with God.

Such Was I

Growing up in a Christian home, I found it easy to trust in myself and my generally moral behavior. I never got in trouble like many of my friends. I never caused my parents heartache, other than getting a few mediocre grades. I counted on being a good person to gain me acceptance with God. I went to church. I had a loving family. I lived a storybook life.

But even such an outwardly reputable life was not enough to commend me to God. I fit the bill of being the hardest person to reach with the gospel. I needed to be born again but did not

40

know it. Though I had the acclaim of my peers, I needed to be born again—just like you.

Meet Nicodemus

Nicodemus was one of the most respected men of his day. He had risen to the top rung of the ladder in God's chosen nation of Israel and had everything going for him. He had a brilliant mind and a head full of spiritual knowledge. He lived a life separated from gross immoralities. He had praise heaped upon him from his many peers. No one would have suspected that someone this upright would need a new life from God. Nicodemus certainly never surmised it. But the new birth is *exactly* what he needed.

The third chapter in the Gospel of John records the personal encounter Nicodemus had with Jesus. This intriguing narrative begins, "Now there was a man of the Pharisees, named Nicodemus, a ruler of the Jews" (John 3:1). Who was this highly revered individual? Who was this man so self-assured about his relationship with God? As we probe into the details of his life, we discover the timeless profile of many people today who never suspect their personal need for the new birth.

The first thing we are told about Nicodemus is that he was a Pharisee. This designation reveals that he was a member of the most spiritually elite group in Israel. The word *Pharisee* means "a separatist," which identified him with a morally and socially isolated group. The Pharisees tried to live as far removed from the moral defilements of the decaying culture as possible. As a Pharisee, Nicodemus was part of the strictest religious sect in the nation and the most conservative party in the land.

Religiously speaking, no one was further to the right than Nicodemus. As a hyper-fundamentalist, he rigidly distanced himself from every sinful influence in the surrounding society. He dug a moat around himself and pulled up the drawbridge. He all but had fellowship with himself alone. Like someone today isolating themselves from the pollutions of society to protect their own holiness, his separation was an outworking of pride. His problem was not on the outside—it was on the inside.

Nicodemus concluded, rightly so, that the moral foundation of their nation was eroding. As a member of this right-wing faction, he feared that their country was drifting away from its spiritual roots. He saw the decadence in the society around them. His misplaced solution was to withdraw in order to remain pure before God. Little did he realize that the real problem lay within himself. He was blind to his own inward corruption.

Separated from Undesirables

As a Pharisee, Nicodemus understood that bad company corrupts good morals. This realization drove him to escape the contaminating influence of the notorious sinners around him. He reasoned that anyone who rubbed shoulders with tax collectors, prostitutes, and thieves would become infected with the deadly plague of their contagious sin. At all costs, he avoided any contact with the lowest dregs of society. He quarantined himself from such deplorables and inoculated himself from the undesirables who were all around him.

But this self-righteous leader had no comprehension that he suffered from the same fatal disease of indwelling sin. He had no self-knowledge of his own depravity. He was thankful he was not like other people. He looked down his long self-righteous nose at others.

Nicodemus was the embodiment of all that Pharisaism represented. But despite maintaining this respectable front, he still felt a gnawing emptiness on the inside. The more he regulated his own conduct, the more restless he became. What could possibly be missing from his highly moral life?

A Rising National Leader

Moreover, Nicodemus was "a ruler of the Jews" (v. 1). This means that he was a member of the Sanhedrin, the inner circle that functioned as the ruling body of the nation. Such an elevated position placed him within the most influential group in Israel. He had climbed the political ladder to the highest level and reached the pinnacle of the country's power structure. In the eyes of everyone, Nicodemus had arrived at the top.

The only people qualified to be part of the Sanhedrin were seventy highly successful men, plus the high priest. This top tier of distinguished leaders held sway as the governing body over Israel. They wielded the ultimate authority in legal and judicial matters. The Sanhedrin was the established power block, much like combining the Supreme Court and Senate of the United States into one ruling body. Whatever verdict this influential group rendered affected the entire nation.

Yet the higher Nicodemus rose, the more something remained wrong. The greater his status, the emptier he felt. The more he achieved, the less he enjoyed it. His power and prestige brought him only mere passing pleasure. The thrill of his worldly success was fleeting and soon left him. His achievements were like biting into cotton candy. They were sweet for a moment but were without substance. Unknown to him, he was discovering that a material world could not fulfill the desires of his longing heart. A pay raise or blossoming ministry could not give inner peace with God. Where must he look for what was missing?

Maybe you can relate to this. Perhaps in your past, the more of the world you gained, the less appealing it became to you. You soon discovered the emptiness of worldly gain and fame. Maybe that is where you presently are. If so, then you can relate to where this man was.

A Strict Bible-Believer

In addition, Nicodemus held strongly conservative beliefs about the Scriptures. The Pharisees were known for taking Scripture literally and strictly. They believed that the written word of God was divinely inspired. Every word had proceeded out of the mouth of God. This means that Nicodemus took the Bible at face value. Like the other Pharisees, he believed in the sovereignty of God over world affairs. He upheld the doctrines of divine predestination and the overruling providence of God— His command of rulers and involvement in every detail of life.

He believed the Bible when it said, "The king's heart is like channels of water in the hand of the LORD; He turns it wherever He wishes" (Prov. 21:1). As an arch-fundamentalist, Nicodemus maintained the final resurrection at the end of the age. He believed in a future kingdom of God upon the earth. With unwavering conviction, he was convinced of the eternal destiny of every soul in either heaven or hell.

A Die-Hard Literalist

Nicodemus was as orthodox as anyone could be. He did not allegorize the Bible, nor did he try to explain it away. He took

Scripture in a straightforward manner. Unlike the Sadducees, who were the religious liberals of the day, he did not deny the reality of the supernatural world. Nor did he doubt the realm of angels, miracles, and the resurrection as the Sadducees did. To the contrary, he believed these biblical matters to be exactly as God had them recorded in His word.

Who would have ever imagined that a Bible-believing, highly esteemed leader like Nicodemus needed a new life from God? Certainly not Nicodemus. But merely agreeing with these doctrines does not place anyone in right standing before God. Even the demons believe these truths and tremble. Tragically, Nicodemus possessed a rigid, dead orthodoxy. He had a full head but an empty heart. He knew about God intellectually but did not know Him personally. He was devoid of saving faith.

The same could be true of any so-called religious person today. Mere head knowledge does not guarantee salvation. Nor does public service or charitable works. An unchanged heart can easily coexist with a learned mind. Could this be describing you?

The Leading Bible Teacher

In their encounter, Jesus addressed Nicodemus as "the teacher of Israel" (John 3:10). That is a high recognition from the Lord Himself. Jesus acknowledged that this respected man was *the* premier Bible teacher in the entire nation. To achieve such a high reputation in Israel meant that he was a foremost expert in the written word. He earned respect for his command of the law. He possessed an astute grasp of the divine precepts. As a preeminent instructor, Nicodemus held the final word on what any biblical passage meant.

Despite his accumulated knowledge, he remained spiritually ignorant of his own need for the new birth. Though he could not put his finger on what was missing, he knew he needed something more than what he possessed with his impressive résumé. What he longed for remained outside of himself. Yet he did not know what it was.

Unknown to Nicodemus, what he needed was God Himself. He needed the spiritual life that only God can give. Despite his vast Bible knowledge, he did not know the most basic truths about how to enter the kingdom of God. Though people had elevated Nicodemus to the lofty status of being the leading Bible scholar, he remained ignorant of the most basic gospel truths. He had outward religion, yet was without any inward reality. Spiritually speaking, he was a dead man walking.

Few Would Suspect It

To observe Nicodemus, none of his peers would suspect he needed to be born again. Not even Nicodemus could discern this. His religious façade was too hard to penetrate with human eyes. His biblical knowledge concealed his unregenerate state. His extensive ministry involvement reinforced the delusion of his right status with God. It was too difficult for others to detect his spiritual emptiness. But underneath this veneer of respectable religiosity, his life was utterly devoid of God. Tragically, he had convinced himself of a spiritual relationship with God that he did not possess.

Nicodemus stands as a prime example of someone who can cognitively know many facts about the Bible but not personally know God and can be so close to the kingdom of God yet so far away from it. He shows that we can be highly religious yet entirely lost. As it was with Nicodemus, so it is with countless people today. We can memorize Scripture, know sound doctrine, and even teach others but not be truly right with God. This restless, empty search for fulfillment pictures what so many of us experience in our striving to be religious. We can pursue an outward morality as the means to gain a right standing before God. But these self-regenerating efforts can never earn us the acceptance we desperately need with Him.

Models of Virtue

Such individuals see themselves as good people. On a human level, they appear to be admirable. They are well-acquainted with the Bible. They use the right vocabulary and sound spiritual in conversations. They are extremely dedicated in their religious service. They are esteemed in the eyes of others for their virtue. They are admired for their wholesome values. But these are the people who most seriously need to see their need for new life from God. They simply do not know what is missing.

These impressive individuals appear as exemplary models of respectable living. They often worship in close association with true believers. They attend Bible studies and even pray with others. They are often highly engaged in ministry and may even be in positions of spiritual leadership. They are esteemed by others for the way they conduct themselves. They have the highest regard for the divine origin of the Bible. They are orthodox in their beliefs. They affirm many of the cardinal truths of Scripture.

But despite their theological orthodoxy, they are oblivious to what they most need but do not have. They have everything except the one elusive thing they most need. What they do not possess is eternal life. This is a dangerous place to be. People in this state of self-deception are counterfeit believers who live in a masquerade world. They can't see their own distance from God. Simply put, these people do not know that they do not know God.

The Pharisees Are Still with Us

Countless multitudes are like this today. They attend church and serve in ministry. They lecture in seminaries and stand in pulpits. They serve in the nursery and teach in Sunday school rooms. They are fine, upstanding citizens who have never committed a serious crime. They have never been part of any sordid business affairs. They have never attempted any underhanded transactions. They keep their distance from questionable places of entertainment. They strive to live pure lives.

But despite being removed from overt practices of sin, they still have an internal problem. Their strict religious practices cannot give them what they so desperately need. A thin veil of morality lies on the surface of their sinful lives. All the while, their souls remain spiritually dead. They are reformed but have never been reborn. They have adhered to a strict code of morality but have never had their hearts changed by God. What they urgently need is eternal life.

Full Heads, Empty Hearts

Untold numbers of people are self-deceived like this. People can have a head full of doctrinal truths, a biblical worldview, the standing of a model citizen, a reputation as religious, and even church status as a leader. In their own eyes, they are in good standing in the family of God. But here is the sad reality: they do not possess eternal life.

These highly moralistic individuals presume that their knowledge of spiritual truths makes them right with God and their many activities have gained them a privileged position with Him. They think they can tally up their good works and present a winning score to God. Even subconsciously, they think they are in a better spiritual standing before Him than the person who has a "losing" score. But God's holy standards are too unattainable for anyone to meet the mark and earn salvation. Our own works can never produce the life of God within us. Our personal striving can never create eternal life in our spiritually dead souls.

The Need Is the Same

No matter where we are in life, whether we are a criminal in prison or a member in fine standing at our church, we share the exact same need. We need the divine grace that alone can regenerate our empty hearts. The Bible says,

> He saved us, not on the basis of deeds which we have done in righteousness, but according to His mercy, by the washing of regeneration and renewing by the Holy Spirit, whom He poured out upon us richly through Jesus Christ our Savior, so that being justified by His grace we would be made heirs according to the hope of eternal life. (Titus 3:5–7)

All people must come to the same place before a holy God. We must come to see our need to be born again. No one is too sinful to be beyond the saving power of God. Nor is anyone so good that they do not need it. This is the truth Nicodemus had to learn.

Maybe you were once like this. Maybe you were once a respected businessperson who donated to charity, attended church regularly, and even led family devotions. Or maybe you were an outwardly faithful spouse and parent, keeping an orderly and moral home. Perhaps you thought of yourself as a good person who assumed that you possessed a relationship with God. Maybe you once lived blind to your unconverted state. Maybe you attended church and presumed everything was fine between you and God. You did many good things for others. You were a straight arrow if ever there was one. But you were self-deceived about where you stood with God. You lived without seeing your need to be born again.

Could you even now be self-deceived about where you stand with the Lord? Could you be presuming on a salvation you have never personally possessed? Many will face this terrifying realization when they stand before the Lord on the last day. Think carefully about the condition of your own soul while the door of opportunity stands open.

A Time for Self-Examination

Maybe you know a lot of truth about the Bible but do not know the One of whom it speaks. Maybe you have a head full of knowledge but a heart empty of God. Perhaps you know certain facts about Jesus Christ but have never placed your faith in Him. Or it could be that you are riding on the coattails of your parents' faith or trusting in your church membership.

Could it be that you come to church but have never come to faith in Jesus Christ? Could it be that you verbally profess faith in Jesus but do not inwardly possess Him? Maybe you have attempted to live a pure life. But despite all your striving, you are yet outside the kingdom of God. You do not need one more book to put on the shelf, one more shallow self-help principle to follow, or one more ministry in which to invest your time. You still fall short of perfection—what God demands.

The Bible is abundantly clear that a right relationship with God is gained not by what we do but by what He does for us in Christ.

> But God, being rich in mercy, because of His great love with which He loved us, even when we were dead in our transgressions, made us alive together with Christ (by grace you have been saved). (Eph. 2:4–5)

Needing God to Work

Entrance into the kingdom is realized in what God does for us. From start to finish, the new birth is the exclusive work of God in us. We cannot save ourselves. We must realize that we contribute nothing to what Jesus Christ has accomplished. God must convict our heart of our own sin. He must create within each of us a hunger and thirst for His perfect righteousness. God must freely give what we so desperately need. He alone can give us a new heart and a new start with Him.

Until this miracle of the new birth occurs within us, each of us remains the hardest person to reach with the gospel. Not one of us will be saved until we know we are lost. Not one of us will seek grace until we see our need of it. Not one of us will believe the good news until we know the bad news about ourselves. Without God's intervention, we are all like Nicodemus, stranded without hope. You may be someone who thinks they understand truth but has not experienced its saving power. When God gives you a new heart, he transforms your affections so that you love Him and desire to obey Him.

Has this happened in your life?

four

Divine Appointment

This man came to Jesus by night and said to Him, "Rabbi, we know that You have come from God as a teacher; for no one can do these signs that You do unless God is with him."

JOHN 3:2

Every personal encounter with Jesus Christ is a divine appointment, an arranged rendezvous preplanned by God. Such a direct meeting is always sovereignly orchestrated by the invisible hand of God. Whenever a person comes face-to-face with the Lord, it is at the divinely set time and in the divinely appointed place. It is never random, never haphazard, never by mere chance or blind fate.

Such is always the case when I am sitting on an airplane and working on a manuscript for a sermon or book. The person seated next to me will inevitably ask me why I am working so hard. This, in turn, leads to a discussion of what I am writing and gives me a wide-open door to witness the gospel to them. These conversations are not by accident. Nor are they chance occurrences. In those moments, I know that these are divine appointments, intended by God for each person to hear about the Lord Jesus Christ. This encounter was scripted by God long ago and brought to pass by the hand of providence.

The Predetermined Plan of God

So it was for Nicodemus the night he approached Jesus. Though he initiated contact, this, nevertheless, was far from a random meeting. This meeting had been set up by God before time began. It was divinely appointed in order for Nicodemus to meet the Lord. Quite simply, this was Nicodemus's time of reckoning with Jesus Christ.

Solomon records, "The mind of man plans his way, but the LORD directs his steps" (Prov. 16:9). Although we plan our path, it is God who orders the way we go. Proverbs also says, "Many plans are in a man's heart, but the counsel of the LORD will stand" (19:21). Regardless what people may purpose, the sovereign will of God will come to pass. This is admittedly a deep and complex subject, but it is nonetheless true. "Man's steps are ordained by the LORD, how then can man understand his way?" (20:24). The lines of providence intersect far above our heads and are beyond our understanding.

The premier example of this is the crucifixion of Jesus Christ. This was the darkest hour in human history. It was the first-degree, premeditated murder of the Son of God. It was the most heinous crime ever committed by godless hands. Certainly, Judas betrayed Him. The Jews called for His death. The Romans performed the execution. Yet this evil deed was "by the predetermined plan and foreknowledge of God" (Acts 2:23).

All the events in this world unfold according to this foreordained plan. What sinful people intend for evil, God means for good (Gen. 50:20). It was God Himself who delivered over His Son unto death (Rom. 4:25; 8:32). Even my own first interaction with the gospel—taught in our home by my parents—was by God's sovereign appointment. The eternal purpose of God steers every event of human history to its appointed end. And this midnight meeting between Nicodemus and Jesus was nothing less than an extraordinarily designed appointment.

A Private Meeting by Night

As we carefully examine this encounter between Nicodemus and Jesus Christ, we read, "This man came to Jesus by night and said to Him, 'Rabbi, we know that You have come from God as a teacher; for no one can do these signs that You do unless God is with him'" (John 3:2). That Nicodemus came "by night" might seem like an incidental detail, but it was intentionally recorded by John. Why does this biblical text make mention of this? What is its significance? There are three primary reasons that stand out.

First, Nicodemus came by night in order to conceal this private meeting from others who knew him. It was not politically correct for Nicodemus to be seen approaching Jesus to learn from Him. If people knew of this meeting, they could have discredited Nicodemus's teaching ministry. He would lose face in the nation. He would no longer be considered *the* teacher of Israel.

Second, if people saw Nicodemus coming to Jesus, it would
have tarnished the reputation of the entire body of the Pharisees. After all, they were the spiritual elitists. For this encounter
to be known would have dealt a blow to their highly protected
reputation. The Pharisees hailed from Jerusalem, the religious
capital of the nation. This was the headquarters of their spiritual
power structure. But Jesus was not from Jerusalem. He was from
lowly Nazareth. There was even a popular saying, "Can any good
thing come out of Nazareth?" (1:46). Everyone looked down
on Nazareth. It was considered the other side of the tracks and
certainly was not in the recognized circle of power for Israel.
No one believed a Pharisee would approach a Nazarite. Nicodemus had to approach Jesus by night in order to conceal this
private meeting.

Third, the apostle John has a deeper meaning in mind. In
the Gospel of John, darkness represents humanity's spiritual
ignorance of God. It also portrays living in the habitual pursuit of sin (3:18–20). Nicodemus coming by night is intended
to portray that he lived in the darkness of his sin. That he
came by night conveys that he came in sheer unbelief. Here
was a person blinded in the darkness of spiritual ignorance
and moral depravity. He was living in a darkened lifestyle
of pervasive sin. He was like any self-deceived sinner today,
self-absorbed and "having no hope and without God in the
world" (Eph. 2:12).

Because Nicodemus lived in spiritual darkness within his
soul, he did not yet understand the true depth of his own depravity. Nor did he know the divine solution in the new birth.
At this point, all he knew was that he was missing something.
But what that was, he did not know. Perhaps Jesus could tell
him.

This is not a dilemma unique to Nicodemus. Everyone born into this world is born into the same blackened state. We all once lived in the darkness, living a life of sin, taking pleasure in evil. This may even still be true in your life, as you read these pages. The Bible says every unconverted person lives in spiritual darkness (Rom. 1:21). Elsewhere, Scripture says, "The god of this world has blinded the minds of the unbelieving so that they might not see the light of the gospel of the glory of Christ" (2 Cor. 4:4). All unbelievers are "darkened in their understanding" (Eph. 4:18).

A Respectful Address

As Nicodemus addressed Jesus, this religious leader spoke most respectfully to Him. He called Him "Rabbi," a title of high honor, meaning "teacher." This formal designation acknowledged Jesus as rightly teaching the law of Moses. People usually addressed Nicodemus as "Rabbi," but now he addressed Jesus as "Rabbi." By this, Nicodemus acknowledged that Jesus was a gifted teacher who possessed a far greater authority than he did.

Though people regarded Nicodemus as a preeminent teacher of Israel, he understood that he was approaching one of a higher rank. Nicodemus had come to inquire of Jesus in order to be taught by Him. He did not recognize the full reality of who Jesus was, but he did realize that Jesus had answers he did not have to the spiritual emptiness in his heart. Whatever Jesus would say, he must listen. After all, Jesus emphatically claimed to be "the truth" (John 14:6). He asserted, "I did not speak on My own initiative, but the Father Himself who sent Me has given Me a commandment as to what to say and what to speak. . . . I speak just as the Father has told Me" (12:49–50). This being so, Nicodemus must give strictest attention to what Jesus taught.

With each step, Nicodemus drew closer to the truth, though he was not yet there. He still did not know the basics of the faith. Jesus was not merely a teacher come from God. Quite the contrary—He was God who had come to teach. A world of difference separates those two statements. The first recognizes Jesus to be on equal footing with the other prophets and teachers. All the prophets of the Old Testament were sent by God. Even John the Baptist came from God (1:6). At this point, Nicodemus saw Jesus as merely one more gifted teacher in a long line of prophets with wise and helpful instruction.

But Nicodemus had not yet recognized the most important truth about Jesus. He failed to discern that Jesus possessed eternal deity in His sinless humanity. In Jesus's incarnation, He willingly laid aside His heavenly glory to inhabit a human body in the form of a lowly servant. Jesus was God in human flesh, truly God yet truly man. As the God-man, He came to accomplish the salvation of sinners. He came on a divine rescue mission to seek and save the lost (Luke 19:10). Nicodemus had not yet seen his need to surrender his life to the lordship of Jesus Christ. But he had come to the right person in search of the truth—for reasons he did not yet understand.

A Spiritually Blinded Mind

Being in darkness, Nicodemus remained without spiritual sight. He did not recognize that standing right in front of him was God in human flesh. He was looking into the face of the eternal Son of God, but Nicodemus was seeing with only physical eyes. He was unable to perceive the true identity of Jesus. Nicodemus was a blind leader of the blind. He was unaware he had come to the long-awaited Messiah. He could not detect that this was the One foretold by the prophecies he had studied.

Nicodemus was standing directly before the only entrance leading into the kingdom of God. Yet his blindness kept him outside it. His feet stood right up against the narrow gate. But he had not taken the decisive step of faith to enter through it. Though a religious leader, Nicodemus remained a foreigner to the kingdom of God. He was on the outside looking in. He was a stranger and an alien to grace.

At this point, Nicodemus recognized Jesus as merely a miracle-working religious teacher. He acknowledged, "no one can do these signs that You do unless God is with him" (John 3:2). Each miracle that Jesus performed was indisputable evidence that God was with Him. Nicodemus referred to these miracles as "signs," which means that he understood there was a spiritual significance attached to them. He perceived there was a greater meaning behind these displays of power by Jesus. But what was it?

Each miracle Jesus performed was a divine confirmation that He had been sent by God. Each display of power validated that He had come to bring salvation to those who were perishing in their sins. When Jesus opened physically blind eyes, He demonstrated that He gives sight to those in spiritual darkness. When He unstopped physically deaf ears, He showed that He gives hearing to those who cannot understand spiritual truth. When He healed paralyzed legs, He showed He could cause sinners to walk in newness of life. Each miracle testified that Jesus gives eternal life, the very thing Nicodemus needed most.

Turning Water into Wine

In the previous chapter of the Gospel of John, we read the first miracle Jesus performed took place at a wedding he attended in Cana. It is the miracle of turning water into wine (John 2:1–11), the very story that led to my own conversion, when the family of the bride unexpectedly and embarrassingly ran out of wine. So the mother of Jesus intervened in this unfortunate turn of events and asked Jesus to do what only He could.

After an initial rebuttal, Jesus told the servants to fill six water pots with water. Once they did, Jesus instructed them to take the water pots, now filled, to the headwaiter. As they carried the water to the headwaiter, Jesus miraculously turned that dirty water into the purest wine.

Transforming Sinners into Saints

This miracle was a sign (v. 11), meaning it was a display of divine power that pictures a truth. That is to say, it was a miracle with a message. Turning water into wine represented a spiritual truth that far exceeded the physical miracle itself. This act of God portrayed His transforming grace that is shown whenever someone is born again. The greatest miracle is not Jesus turning water into wine. Instead, it is when Jesus transforms a sinner into a saint. This spiritual change is the most radical alteration anyone can possibly experience.

This is what Nicodemus had to come to grips with about his own life. He must be transformed from the dirty water he was into the sparkling wine of a new person. He must be dramatically changed on the inside from what he was into what he must become. The old life in Adam must be replaced by new life in

Christ. Only Jesus can take a sin-stained person such as Nicodemus and change him into who God intends him to be. This
is the abundant life that Jesus came to give. Though Nicodemus
did not realize it yet, this is the miracle he must experience.

A Searching Question

Where are *you* in relation to the kingdom of God? I hope that
you have already entered the kingdom of God. If so, this is what
God has done in your life. But perhaps you have not yet been
born again. If you are outside the kingdom, you need to enter
by the new birth.

Maybe you have chased after the world. Maybe you have pursued mere religion to fill this emptiness. Maybe you have searched
in many places and found nothing to satisfy you. Maybe you have
even tried church, but it leaves you empty. Maybe you lack the
reality of what only God can give you.

Are you still searching for the one thing that will fill the
empty void in your life? Why is there nothing lasting in what
you continuously strive after? Why do these quests leave you
so restless? What can fill this empty void inside you? What is
this one thing you desperately need?

What Is Missing?

What is sorely missing will not be discovered in the temporal
enjoyments of this world, and what you are searching for will
not be found within you. What you need comes from outside of
you—even from outside of this world. The answer you are looking for must come from a *higher* source. What you are searching
for is found in God and what only He can give.

Instead of hiding under the cover of spiritual darkness like Nicodemus, you are called by God to come to faith in His Son. Come to the Lord Jesus Christ. You must see your need for the life He offers. You must turn away from your empty religious trappings and come to the saving knowledge of Jesus Christ. Today, He says to you:

> Come to Me, all who are weary and heavy-laden, and I will give you rest. Take My yoke upon you and learn from Me, for I am gentle and humble in heart, and you will find rest for your souls. For My yoke is easy and My burden is light. (Matt. 11:28–30)

A Pressing Need

What each of us needs is an entirely new life from God. We were created by Him in His own image. He is the One who gave us physical life. He alone can give us spiritual life. Only God can satisfy our empty souls with eternal life and impart new life to our dead hearts. Until we receive a new heart, our innermost being will always remain empty and restless.

What about you? Are you desperately searching for something? Or is it Someone? What you need is for God to give you eternal life. God has put eternity within your soul. This means your inner longings can only be satisfied by the One who put them there. Early theologian Augustine once noted, "Our hearts are restless until they find their rest in You." He was right. Until your soul finds rest in God, you will remain restless—forever.

In these chapters, I want to show you how Jesus explained this truth to Nicodemus. Maybe you stand exactly where Nicodemus once stood. Though he could not see the kingdom, he was near it.

five

Shocking News

Jesus answered and said to him, "Truly, truly, I say to you, unless one is born again he cannot see the kingdom of God."

JOHN 3:3

Have you ever received unexpected news that hits you hard? A stunning report that leaves you speechless? A shocking update that jolts you to the core of your being? When you least expect it and when you are least prepared to receive it, you are told the very opposite of what you expect to hear. The message causes you to lose all equilibrium, leaving you speechless.

I will never forget receiving one such shocking report that hit me like a semitruck. My father, brother, sister, and I were in my mother's hospital room, waiting for her to be returned from having surgery. When she had been wheeled out of her room earlier for the surgery, she was laughing with us. But later, when the surgeon reentered the room, the atmosphere completely changed. He told my father to sit down and said he had hard news for him to hear. He'd discovered that my mother had such an aggressive cancer that she had only months to live.

As we heard this unexpected news, we were stunned. Afterward, my father and I drove home in deafening silence, reeling from the blow. We had no words to speak to each other.

This earth-shattering report was something like what Nicodemus felt when Jesus abruptly addressed him that night. What this religious leader heard was the last thing he expected to hear. He presumed he had a right standing with God and an elevated status in the kingdom of God. Though he suspected something was missing, he never expected it was this serious. What he was about to be told was a total contradiction of everything he had ever believed about himself.

Cutting to the Chase

With heart-piercing words, Jesus cut straight to the chase. He said to Nicodemus, "Truly, truly, I say to you, unless one is born again he cannot see the kingdom of God" (John 3:3). In no uncertain words, Jesus stated that if this highly respected man was to see the kingdom of God, he *must* be born again. This message hit Nicodemus like a ton of bricks. Jesus confronted him and announced that his entire life had been a complete failure in the sight of God. The Lord said that Nicodemus needed to start his life all over. This great teacher in the nation knew nothing about true entrance into the kingdom of God.

Undoubtedly, Nicodemus was shocked that this rebuke from Jesus could apply to someone as eminently successful as he was.

It did not seem possible that a religious figure as advanced in the Bible would need to start over with God. But to his utter astonishment, this was precisely what he heard from Jesus. Hard as it was to hear, it was even harder to swallow. Nevertheless, this truth was exactly what this self-righteous man needed to be told.

When Nicodemus approached Jesus, Jesus abruptly answered him before he could even voice one question. Jesus read this spiritual leader like an open book. He saw right through him. With penetrating words, He went straight to the heart of Nicodemus and confronted his dire spiritual need.

Jesus explained that all of Nicodemus's self-righteous deeds had gained him nothing in finding acceptance with God. With laser-like insight, the Lord looked past his admirable façade and peered into his sin-tainted heart. Jesus immediately audited his soul and calculated the spiritual bankruptcy of this religious leader.

The Lord went directly to the bottom line and asserted what must take place in this highly respected man's life. Jesus mandated the necessity of the new birth. This was non-negotiable. If Nicodemus was to see the kingdom of God, the stunning news was that he must be *born again*. Otherwise, he would perish. In our own day, self-righteousness can come in many forms—a trust in one's own morals, church tradition, or even political conservatism. But none of these superficial pursuits can bring salvation or the needed change to start over.

Pay Attention to This

In this private exchange, Jesus spoke directly into Nicodemus's life. He started with these attention-grabbing words, "Truly,

truly." This phrase comes from the Greek word *amēn*, which means "it is so." Jesus was saying, literally, "Amen, amen." Or, "This is true, this is true." This double emphasis was meant to capture and hold Nicodemus's attention, so he would truly hear what would follow.

Then Jesus added, "I say to you." This is as much a direct confrontation as a communication. Jesus spoke to Nicodemus with penetrating focus, as if there was no one else on Planet Earth. This was not directed to "whoever," as Jesus will do later (v. 16). Instead, these words were highly personal, intended specifically for Nicodemus. This is a narrowly aimed arrow, fired directly at the target of his heart.

The same is true when Jesus addresses us in His word. When we hear the call of the gospel, Jesus speaks directly to each of us, as if we are the only person on earth. The divine requirement is that every individual must be born again to enter the kingdom of heaven. There are no exceptions.

The Bottom-Line Assessment

Jesus continued by assessing the spiritual state of Nicodemus's soul. This did not come from one of the other rabbis. This was not the result of an opinion poll taken on the street. Nor was it the findings of a survey of the religious community. Instead, it came straight from the mind of God in human flesh—the Son of God Himself. What did Jesus say?

Some statements that Jesus issued on earth rise to the highest level of critical significance. This is one of those monumental statements. Everything else in Nicodemus's life was reduced to secondary status. At stake was Nicodemus's standing before God. Upon these words hung his everlasting destiny.

To his utter astonishment, Nicodemus heard that *he* must be born again. Jesus said to him, "Unless one is born again he cannot see the kingdom of God" (v. 3). With these heart-shattering, pointed words, Jesus stressed that the new birth is absolutely mandatory for him to enter the kingdom of heaven. If Nicodemus was to see the kingdom of God, he must receive new life from God in his spiritually dead soul. No statement could have been more jolting for this religious leader to hear.

When Jesus said Nicodemus must be "born again," the Greek word translated "again" (*anōthen*) has two basic meanings in the original language. This word often means "anew," or "a second time." For example, the apostle Paul used it this way when he wrote, "How is it that you turn back *again*?" (Gal. 4:9, emphasis added). In this instance, the Galatian believers had been converted under the grace-filled preaching of the apostle Paul. Yet they had turned back "again"—a second time—to where they had been previously living in the flesh. In like manner, when Jesus told Nicodemus he must be "born again," He meant that this religious leader must be born a *second* time. Nicodemus needed more than a physical birth. What he needed was a second birth, a spiritual birth.

Born from Above

This word "again" can also mean "above." It indicates a place that is above and beyond this world. This second birth is also from "above," referring to where God dwells "above" in heaven. Later in this same chapter of John, this Greek word (*anōthen*) is used with this exact meaning. When John writes, "He who comes from *above* is above all" (John 3:31, emphasis added), *anōthen* indicates that Jesus Christ entered this world from *above*.

Jesus came down from the heights of heaven to enter this lowly world. He used this same word when He stood before Pilate: "You would have no authority over Me, unless it had been given you from *above*" (John 19:11, emphasis added). In this passage, Jesus declared that the authority of Pilate was granted from heaven *above*, where eternal God dwells.

The use of "again" stresses the heavenly origin of the new birth. It must come down from a much *higher* realm than this world. Nicodemus must experience a second birth that can only originate from above. His spiritual birth cannot be self-generated, self-manufactured, or self-produced from any of his religious activities or good works. Instead, the new birth must descend from the throne of grace. Simply put, the new birth is an out-of-this-world experience.

An Indictment of Our First Birth

The fact that we must be born again is a stinging indictment of our first birth, which was marred by our inherited sin nature. David writes, "Behold, I was brought forth in iniquity, and in sin my mother conceived me" (Ps. 51:5). This statement does not mean that David's conception in his mother's womb was a sinful act. Rather, it teaches that the sinful nature of Adam was transmitted to David at the moment of his conception. A preset bent toward evil was passed down from his forefather Adam. This is not simply true just of David but of every person ever conceived.

Because every person received a sin nature, we each come forth from our mother's womb able to commit sinful acts. David states, "The wicked are estranged from the womb; these who speak lies go astray from birth" (58:3). This means that Nicodemus—and every member of the human race—entered this world with a radically corrupt sin nature. This religious ruler came forth at birth pursuing sin and speaking lies. This is why the new birth is so necessary for him—and for us.

The Teaching of Total Depravity

From cover to cover, the Bible teaches the total depravity of every person. This explains the complete saturation of our souls with sin. The prophet Jeremiah writes, "The heart is more deceitful than all else and is desperately sick; who can understand it?" (Jer. 17:9). In other words, there are evil desires bound up in every heart. This lust for sin is so deeply embedded in human nature that no one can grasp the full magnitude of how inherently corrupt it is. Nicodemus was no different.

Elsewhere, Solomon states that "the hearts of the sons of men are full of evil and insanity" (Eccles. 9:3). Solomon pursued wealth and women instead of wisdom to satisfy himself at the end of his life. He wrote Ecclesiastes to recount the vanity and emptiness of life apart from God. He knew well the depravity of the heart. This verse teaches that every person's heart is plagued with evil. The carnal mind is "full of insanity," meaning it is unable to grasp spiritual truth and the right course of action. There are no exceptions to this. Not even Nicodemus.

Where does this put him? By all outward appearances, if anyone did not need to be born again, it was Nicodemus. If anyone could have been granted a special exemption from this strict requirement, it would have been this man, who was a paragon of religiosity. This precise man was firmly committed to the moral law of the Old Testament and meticulous in every attempt to keep the exact letter of the divine word.

He looked as blameless as anyone could be. He appeared to be a role model of purity. Mothers would have wanted their sons to grow up to be like him. They would have wanted their daughters to marry someone like him. However, Nicodemus, though strictly moral, could not meet the divine standard of perfection. Even a seemingly good person like Nicodemus must be born again.

From his conception, the deadly poison of sin had already permeated his every faculty, marring his mind, affections, and will. All humankind is born estranged from God. We are predisposed to rebel against Him. This is why the new birth is so imperative.

The Problem of the Heart

Jesus taught this when He said: "For from within, out of the heart of men, proceed the evil thoughts, fornications, thefts, murders, adulteries, deeds of coveting and wickedness, as well as deceit, sensuality, envy, slander, pride and foolishness. All these evil things proceed from within and defile the man" (Mark 7:21–23). The human heart is full of all kinds of unlawful sins. It has been said that the heart of the human problem is the problem of the human heart. This sobering diagnosis by the Lord Jesus traces all sin back to the heart.

Other passages likewise teach that every person who enters this world is spiritually dead. Paul bluntly asserts, "You were dead in your trespasses and sins" (Eph. 2:1). This teaches that everyone outside the kingdom of God is devoid of any spiritual life. Again, the apostle affirms, "You were dead in your transgressions" (Col. 2:13), recounting the spiritual state of all people before regeneration. This states that everyone is conceived without any spiritual life in their mother's womb. Therefore, every individual must receive the spiritual life that only comes from the second birth.

The Moral Inability of Man

When Jesus declared to Nicodemus, "Unless one is born again he cannot see the kingdom of God" (John 3:3), the word *cannot* leaps off the page. If Jesus had merely said "may not," it would have meant that he needed permission by Him to be born again. It would mean all that was needed was an open invitation by Jesus. That the new birth could be consciously stepped into by Nicodemus is not what Jesus is saying. To the contrary, the word *cannot* stresses the moral inability of Nicodemus. *Cannot* indicates one's lack of any ability to affect one's new birth. Nicodemus cannot be born again and enter the kingdom by anything he does. The difference between cannot and may not is vast. Jesus was insisting that Nicodemus did not have the capacity to birth himself into this spiritual kingdom.

As already noted, Nicodemus did nothing to contribute to his first birth. In like manner, he could do nothing to contribute to his second birth. The new birth is accomplished exclusively by God. No matter how upright we may appear to be, it will never contribute to us receiving new life from God.

The Right Diagnosis and the Only Cure

It has been said that a right diagnosis is half the cure. If so, here is the right diagnosis, issued by the Great Physician, and this grim report by Jesus was brutally accurate. No one had ever addressed Nicodemus so directly. In this one statement, Jesus

71

demolished the self-inflated view Nicodemus had of himself. With this one assessment, Christ ripped off his religious façade and stripped away the thin veneer of his superficial hypocrisy to expose Nicodemus's spiritual condition, in which he falsely assumed that he was right with God.

Here is what was so troubling. These words put Nicodemus on the same spiritual plane as everyone else. Jesus said that he had no special status before God. Though a leading figure in the religious establishment, *he*, nevertheless, must be born again. This placed Nicodemus where he would have never expected to be: just as spiritually bankrupt as the beggars and prostitutes he despised. There was no special exemption granted to him. He was not shown a side door by which he could enter the kingdom.

By insisting upon the new birth, Jesus told Nicodemus that he must spiritually start over. To this point, all his religious activities had counted for nothing toward obtaining God's favor. His self-righteousness was valued to be worthless. The supposed deposits he had been making with God had been fool's gold. Nicodemus had to come to the end of himself. He had to realize there was nothing he could do to gain entrance into the kingdom of God.

This stinging rebuke by Jesus was utterly devastating for Nicodemus to hear. He had *never* heard a report like this. There was nothing he could do to produce his spiritual birth. God alone could spark new life in his cold, unregenerate heart. By this divine act, God must do what Nicodemus could not do for himself. In the new birth, Jesus said that God must conceive life in Nicodemus's spiritually dead soul.

If you are born again, you should give unending praise to God that you find yourself birthed into His kingdom. It is nothing less than a divinely performed miracle that we have been made alive in Christ. God has intervened in our life and done for us what we could never do for ourselves. Every Christian is a living miracle, wrought by the omnipotent hands of God.

This life-giving reality should be of great encouragement to us in our witnessing the gospel to others. No matter how resistant a person may be to the truth, God is abundantly able to cause them to be born again. No one is beyond the power of God to birth them into His kingdom. In every new birth, God intervenes and overcomes the unbelief in a human's heart.

What about You?

Have *you* been born again? No more critical question could be put before you. Maybe you are not quite sure what your answer is. If that is your case, I urge you, then, to hear the teaching of Jesus Christ that is being laid before you. If you have never been born again, pray and ask God to give you this new life.

No matter how religious you may be, you *must* be born again. You may have family members who are born again or friends who have received this new life. You may attend a church that rightly teaches the new birth—you may even be devoutly religious and associate with genuine Christians. But none of these is a substitute for you being born again. Regardless of your religious standing or social status, your greatest need is to experience this new birth. You must experience this spiritual resurrection in your life. There is no other way to see God's kingdom except through this supernatural miracle. There is no other way to gain entrance into the realm of salvation. If you are to enter the kingdom of heaven, you must be born from above.

A Word to Believers

If you are a Christian, consider the richness of the new birth in Christ and the miracle of this life-changing reality. Your heart—spiritually made warm, living flesh instead of cold, hard stone. All your sins—forgiven. Instead of your previous slavery to sin, you now have new life in Christ. You have a new heart to love Christ and serve Him. God has turned your heart to Him, and He has given you faith to believe in His Son. You should give glory to God for performing such a miracle in your soul.

The new birth does not give you a mere upgrade of your old life. God has given you an entirely new life, one unlike anything you have ever previously experienced. What a glorious truth!

six

Heart Transplant

Jesus answered and said to him, "Truly, truly, I say to you, unless one is born again he cannot see the kingdom of God."

JOHN 3:3

Early in my ministry, an aspiring young surgeon moved to the city where I was pastoring and joined our church. This brilliant physician relocated for the specific purpose of starting his first medical practice. His hope was to perform the first heart transplant surgery in the history of the state. Possessing a razor-sharp mind and skilled hands, this young doctor had been trained by the best heart transplant doctors in the world to perform this life-saving operation.

Soon thereafter, this gifted surgeon received a patient who was suffering from a failing heart. The diagnosis was that she desperately needed a new heart or she would not live much longer. The need for a heart donor was made known, and the day came when an organ donor who had agreed to leave her heart to someone in need died.

A team of doctors carefully harvested the heart from the donor. This blood-pumping muscle was placed inside a cooler and kept in ice. The cooler was then put in an ambulance and rushed to the airport, where a charter jet was waiting to fly the heart hundreds of miles away, to our city. When the plane landed, an emergency vehicle was on the tarmac, ready to receive this precious gift. The cooler containing the heart was placed into the ambulance and sped to the hospital, where the physician, assisted by another physician and a team of medical staff, was waiting to perform the delicate procedure.

Lying on the operating table was the patient with the malfunctioning heart. The ice chest was hurried into the operating room and placed next to the dying woman. The long-awaited moment had come. The healthy heart was ready to be transplanted into its new recipient.

The Great Exchange

This highly trained heart surgeon first opened the chest cavity of his dying patient. He made the necessary incisions and removed the failing heart. He then warmed the chilled heart and placed it inside the patient's chest. With precise stitches, this physician connected the new heart to the aorta and the other blood vessels. The heart was given an electrical shock, which jump-started its beating. Suddenly, the new heart began producing blood.

This young surgeon then closed up the patient's chest with a series of stitches. The next hours and days would reveal if the procedure was successful. The heart recipient was moved to the critical care unit to be carefully monitored as all waited to see how her body would respond. After an appropriate recovery time, it was determined that the surgery was effective. This first heart transplant recipient in the state was eventually released to return home with a new heart and a new start in life.

A Spiritual Heart Transplant

This heart transplant surgery provides a vivid picture of what the Bible calls the new birth. Every human being finds themselves where this dying patient was. We all enter this world with a failed spiritual heart, desperately in need of a replacement. To live eternally with God, we all need a new heart. In the new birth, God, the Great Physician, removes our old heart and replaces it with a new heart.

How important is this exchange? What our physical heart is to our body, our spiritual heart is to our soul. Both are necessary to live. As our physical heart supplies blood to every part of our physical existence, so our spiritual heart produces what we need to live the Christian life. As a healthy heart gives blood to our body, a new spiritual heart pumps spiritual life to our soul.

Our heart, spiritually speaking, encompasses our whole innermost being. Our heart is our real self. It includes our mind, emotions, and will. It is where we think, feel, and choose. Our heart is the seat of our human personality, and it is synonymous with our soul. It is the very center of our inner person, what directs and drives our life. It contains our deepest thoughts, secret ambitions, and strongest affections. It includes our fundamental likes and dislikes, our emotions, and our powers of choice. Our heart is who we *really* are.

Nicodemus was a man who desperately needed a heart transplant. By all outward appearances, his heart was in perfect working order. His spiritual pulse seemed to be strong. His heartbeat for the law of God would have produced a perfect EKG. His vital signs for personal purity seemed to signify a healthy heart. However, Jesus revealed Nicodemus's heart was in desperate need of a transplant. Without a new heart, a new life is impossible.

Jesus, the Great Physician of the soul, addressed Nicodemus and said what no one had ever said to him. Jesus told him, point-blank, that despite his exemplary morality and earnest religion, he *must* receive a new heart in the miracle of the new birth.

A New Heart for a New Start

In the new birth, God gives a new heart for a new start in life. This divine operation produces the most positive life change we could ever experience. Being born again removes our old heart and replaces it with a new one. Previously, we had no heart for God. We had no spiritual life within us. But the second birth implanted a new heart for God, which gave us eternal life in our dead souls. The new birth gave us an entirely new life in the depths of our beings.

Long ago, God promised this heart transplant when He spoke through the prophet Ezekiel:

> Then I will sprinkle clean water on you, and you will be clean;
> I will cleanse you from all your filthiness and from all your
> idols. Moreover, I will give you a new heart and put a new spirit
> within you; and I will remove the heart of stone from your flesh
> and give you a heart of flesh. I will put My Spirit within you

and cause you to walk in My statutes, and you will be careful to observe My ordinances. (Ezek. 36:25–27)

In this ancient prophecy, God Himself is the speaker. With great detail, He describes the truth of the new birth. In this divine act, God declares that He will cleanse the sin-polluted soul of a person with pure water. This spiritual washing illustrates the inner cleansing of the Holy Spirit. He removes all the moral filth that has long stained the soul. God then takes out the old heart of stone that was hardened toward Him. This old heart was dead, without any spiritual life. It could not respond to God, nor did it love Him.

In its place, God implants a new heart of flesh that is alive to Him. It possesses a strong heartbeat—a vibrant, spiritual pulse—for God and His Son, Jesus Christ. God then places His Holy Spirit into the new heart to permanently indwell it. The Spirit works deeply within and causes this person to walk a new path of love for God that leads to obedience to His word.

A New Heart from God

This is the new heart that every person needs. Through this miracle, everything is made new. The Bible says, "Therefore if anyone is in Christ, he is a new creature; the old things passed away; behold, new things have come" (2 Cor. 5:17). This new heart has new affections and new desires for God. It has a new priority and new passion for Jesus Christ. This new heart leads in a new direction with a new ambition to glorify God.

Being born again means that God removes our old hearts and puts the past behind us. We are no longer dominated by past vices or previous unbelief. God wipes the slate clean of all our past sins. We are no longer under the condemnation of God that our sins previously brought upon us (Rom. 8:1). God buries the old heart we once had. Our old selves are no longer who we are. The new birth means we receive this new heart as we become entirely new people in Christ. A new day has dawned. A bright future is breaking on the horizon.

This new life in Christ produces a new joy in the Lord, a new obedience to His word, and a new love for other believers. It gives spiritual discernment that recognizes error and imparts a new pursuit of practical righteousness. Moreover, this new life in Christ gives assurance of salvation and leads to answered prayers according to God's will. From top to bottom, it alters every aspect of a person's existence and gives a radically transformed life from the inside out.

A New Heart to Love God

First, the new birth gives us a new heart to love God. The apostle John writes, "For this is the love of God, that we keep His commandments; and His commandments are not burdensome" (1 John 5:3). Our old heart was hardened toward Him. It was a heart of stone that was spiritually dead. It had no vital pulse for the truth of God. It had no capacity to respond to the things of God—spiritually lifeless without true affection for Him. Worse, our old heart was not neutral toward God but resistant to Him and even opposed to Him. Our old self rejected the authority of God and the demands of His law. The people we once were sought after our own desires to sin and for the things of this passing world.

But in the new birth, God implanted within us a new heart. This second heart instills a new love for Him. This exchanged heart possesses new desires for the kingdom of God. It throbs with new affections for the truth of God and beats in sync with God. Now we love what God loves and reject what He rejects. Likewise, we love what we once rejected and reject what we once loved.

A New Heart to Know God

Second, the new birth gives us a new mind to think right thoughts about who God is and how He works in life. The apostle Paul states:

> In reference to your former manner of life, you lay aside the old self, which is being corrupted in accordance with the lusts of deceit, and [are] renewed in the spirit of your mind, and put on the new self, which in the likeness of God has been created in righteousness and holiness of the truth. (Eph. 4:22–24)

This new mind allows us to have an accurate evaluation of ourselves and a right estimate of our relationship with God. Previously, we lived in ignorance of Him. We lived in spiritual darkness and could not grasp the divine truths in Scripture. The gospel was foolishness to us and made no sense to our sin-impaired thinking. The truth of God was incomprehensible to us.

But the new birth gives us a new mind with which we now know God. It gives us the mind of Christ, which enables us to think like Him with an eternal perspective. Being born again gives us an entirely new mindset, and we see life as God sees it. This new vision is like a pair of glasses that allow us to see the truth of the kingdom of God with 20/20 vision. We see the world as it is and can see the narrow path God has for us as we move forward through life.

We are able to see with a new understanding what God is saying in His word. In addition, we now see how divine truth relates to our life. Where we once lived in darkness without the knowledge of God, we now know the truth.

A New Heart to Believe God

Third, the new birth also gives us a new heart to believe what God is saying in His written word. This new heart accepts the truth that, "All Scripture is inspired by God and profitable for teaching, for reproof, for correction, for training in righteousness" (2 Tim. 3:16). We previously lived in unbelief and could not receive the truth. We had a heart that could not trust what God was saying in the Bible. It questioned the veracity of Scripture. It doubted the teaching of the Bible.

But the new birth gives us a new heart that believes the word of God. We are enabled to accept what God is saying in Scripture. We now discern what God means by what He says in His word. This new heart enables us to grasp the message of the word with understanding and instinctively trust what God says in Scripture.

A New Heart to Praise God

Fourth, the new birth gives us a new heart full of praise for God. Previously, our old heart was self-absorbed. As Solomon states, "Do you see a man wise in his own eyes? There is more hope for a fool than for him" (Prov. 26:12). Our old heart was self-centered and self-deceiving. It withheld the glory that belonged to God and sang our own praises. We gloried in ourselves every time we gave ourselves credit for the good things we had done. Instead of acknowledging the Most High God, we hoarded the glory for ourselves.

But the new birth dramatically changed our life. Our new heart began to speak with new praise for God. New words that exalted God came out of our mouth, and wholesome speech now flows from our lips. Our words no longer flatter ourselves. Or if they do, we are convicted about it and repent. Our words no longer tear others down as they once did. And if they do, we experience godly remorse and seek repentance. Praise for God freely flows from our mouth where previously there was only selfish talk. Our words magnify His name while speaking humbly of ourselves.

A New Heart to Obey God

Fifth, the new birth gives us a new heart that leads us down a new path of obedience to God. Jesus says, "If you love Me, you will keep My commandments" (John 14:15). Our old heart carried us down the broad path of disobedience to God's word that is paved with sinful indulgences and carnal pleasures. We previously walked according to the course of this world (Eph. 2:2). We once traveled with many on the broad path to destruction. On this hell-bound journey, we rejected God and served ourselves. We walked in darkness and had no desire to pursue holiness. We journeyed with those who hated the truth and trafficked with those who loved the lies of the world.

But the new birth put a new heart within us that leads us to walk an entirely new path. Our new heart causes us to depart from the broad path we once journeyed. We have broken from the pack and no longer go along with the flow of this world. In a complete reversal, we are now headed in an entirely new direction, against the heavy traffic of this world system. We have a new destination in sight. We now travel with a new crowd on the narrow path of obedience to God. The world is behind us, and heaven is before us.

As you can see, the new birth effects radical change in our life. The creation of new life within us occurs at the deepest level of our innermost being. Being born again brings about a fundamental alteration in who we are and effects an earth-shaking seismic shift in our soul. We, quite literally, become a new person in Christ. The old person we once were is buried and no longer dominates us. Our old life is ancient history. A new life in God has started. We now are alive in Christ and pursuing Him who leads us every step of the way.

What about Your Heart?

Maybe you are where Nicodemus found himself. Maybe you do not yet understand that you need a new heart. Something inside of you, though, is restless. You are unfulfilled by the things of this world. Perhaps you are searching for what is missing in your life. If this describes you, you need what Nicodemus needed—a new heart. And the only way for you to receive a heart transplant is through the new birth. Only then will you receive a new start in life.

Nothing else will satisfy, nothing else will bring peace to the deepest longings of your heart. Every created thing was designed to reflect the greatness of the Creator. He alone is worthy of your heart's devotion, and He alone can bring about this new birth. Leave behind the riches of this world, the false promises prosperity makes. "But seek first His kingdom and His righteousness, and all these things will be added to you" (Matt. 6:33).

Have you already received a new heart from God? If so, learn more about this divine transformation that has occurred in your life and praise Him with joy for your salvation. If you have not experienced this heavenly rebirth, what follows will reveal exactly what you need.

This Dramatic Change

If you have been born again, you will surely see this dramatic change in your life. You are no longer the person you once were but have become a new person in Christ. You have received so much more than forgiveness of sins. You have actually received a new life that changes you at the deepest level of your soul. You have received a heart transplant to love God more than anyone or anything in this world. You have a new heart to obey God and to no longer go your own way and do anything you desire.

Moreover, you have received a new desire to want to know God, no longer content to merely know about Him. You have received a new heart to believe God and trust His word for daily guidance, to praise God and no longer direct attention to yourself.

If you are born again, this is the supernatural transformation God has brought about in your life.

seven

Starting Over

Nicodemus said to Him, "How can a man be born when he is old? He cannot enter a second time into his mother's womb and be born, can he?"

JOHN 3:4

Have you ever been told that you have been wrong about something you have believed your whole life? Consider how stunned you would feel after being told that you have wasted valuable time and energy making strides in the wrong direction. Think about the painful realization of being informed that, to this point, you have accomplished nothing. What would it be like to have nothing to show for all your efforts?

This is how investors feel when they have poured their hard-earned money into a company that unexpectedly goes bankrupt. After years of putting capital into the enterprise, they have no profits to show for it, only losses. This is how a wife feels after she gives herself to her husband for many years and then painfully suffers the rejection of seeing him walk away from the marriage. After much sacrifice, she has nothing to show for it except abandonment. How does such a person start over with her life?

Nicodemus found himself at a similar crossroads after this self-righteous ruler was told by Jesus that he must be born again. In other words, he must completely start over with God. All his years of strict religious living profited him nothing toward entrance into the kingdom of God. All his good works and respectable morality resulted in no standing of acceptance with God. He would have to renounce everything he thought would commend him to God.

Nicodemus must accept this assessment by Jesus, that he had misspent his entire life in pursuing that which would gain him nothing. His religious efforts, spiritual activities, moral pursuits—everything he attempted left him spiritually penniless. He would have to concede that he was wrong all along and swallow his pride. And that is a bitter pill to swallow.

A Stunning Message, An Honest Response

At this very same point, Nicodemus asked the crucial question—*How can I have this new start with God?* There was an intense struggle in his soul to grapple with the truths Jesus presented him. This religious leader has heard that unless he is born again, he cannot even see the kingdom of heaven, much less enter it. The critical question rose immediately to the surface of his mind and came out of his mouth. "How is this even possible? How can I have this new start with God? How can I have this new life?"

This stunning message of the new birth provoked these questions within Nicodemus. The necessity of being born again struck him like a lightning bolt out of heaven. These words were a stinging rebuke of his own complete lack of personal ability to enter the kingdom of God. As he stood, his sinful life barred him from any entrance into the kingdom. If he was to gain admission, he must have a new start with God. Simply put, he must be born again.

In a state of confusion, Nicodemus responded, "How can a man be born when he is old? He cannot enter a second time into his mother's womb and be born, can he?" (John 3:4). By saying this, Nicodemus did not take Jesus's words to mean that he must literally reenter his mother's womb. He did not think that he must be physically born a second time. He knew that was not the intent of Jesus's words. Rather, he rightly surmised that Jesus was speaking metaphorically.

Borrowing this same birthing analogy, Nicodemus meant, "What do you expect me to do? I cannot crawl back into my mother's womb. How would I start over?" Put another way, he was asking, "Please tell me, how do I start over with God?" This was spoken with a note of sincere inquiry. Nicodemus was asking, "What are you trying to say to me? What are you talking about? How can I see the kingdom of God?"

Without a Question Raised

So abrupt were Jesus's words when Nicodemus came to Him that he didn't even have the opportunity to ask his own question. Before this revered expert could begin, Jesus already answered him. He announced, "Truly, truly, I say to you, unless one is born again he cannot see the kingdom of God" (v. 3).

With this bold declaration, Jesus confronted Nicodemus with the sobering reality that he was so ruined by his first birth, he could not see the kingdom of God apart from a second birth.

By this strong pronouncement, Jesus stated that even the best accomplishments Nicodemus could offer God gain him no status with Him. He has no better standing before God than when he entered this world. In fact, he is worse than when he started. His sins have piled up to the heights of heaven. His sins rightly deserve the wrath of God. For all his religious service, he is far removed from the kingdom. Nicodemus has no spiritual life whatsoever. His superficial religion has left him buried in a spiritual grave.

Nicodemus has been put in his place. This is somewhere he has never been before. He must come to grips with this verdict rendered by this itinerate Rabbi. Jesus demands he renounce his inflated estimate of himself. He must see himself as Jesus sees him. This mandate must have made the self-righteous man choke on his own supposed morality.

Will He Believe Jesus?

Here was the issue that confronted Nicodemus: Would he continue to see himself as he always had, as a morally good person who had earned merit with God? Or would he accept the brutally honest assessment by Jesus concerning his barren spiritual account? Would he believe Christ's abrupt audit of his soul? Would he accept that he had nothing with which to commend himself to God? Which estimate of himself would he believe? Would he cling to what he had previously presumed about himself? Or would he receive what Jesus stated?

As Nicodemus pondered this, he had to address an even greater issue: Who exactly was Jesus? Who was this One standing before him? Why should he believe *Him*? The answers that Nicodemus would supply to these questions would dictate whether or not he accepts what he has heard. These are also the answers that determine whether each of us accepts Christ's words.

More Than a Rabbi

To begin with, Nicodemus had already addressed Jesus as "Rabbi" (v. 2), which means "teacher." Further, he had acknowledged that Jesus was not an ordinary teacher. He had "come from God as a teacher" (v. 2). He acknowledged that Jesus was an even greater Teacher than himself. Moreover, Jesus had a special calling from God. Would Nicodemus accept the pronouncement of Jesus upon his life? It stood contrary to what he had believed about himself his whole life. Who *really* is Jesus? It is the decisive question all of us face.

Undoubtedly, Nicodemus had heard about Jesus's commanding authority. In the city of Jerusalem, where Nicodemus lived, Jesus had recently cleansed the temple of its moral corruption (John 2:13–15). By the sheer force of His convictions, Jesus had turned over the tables of the money changers and driven them out with a whip. Further, He claimed the temple to be His Father's house (v. 16). Nicodemus had surely heard about this demonstration of His righteous outrage. In fact, he had surely also heard about Jesus's claim to have a special relationship with God, calling Him His Father (v. 16). He sensed that Jesus was one to whom he should give strict attention. But would he believe that he must be born again?

What about the Miracles?

Moreover, Nicodemus acknowledged that Jesus had performed miracles by the power of God. He had acknowledged, "No one can do these signs that You do unless God is with him" (3:2). He fully accepted that Jesus performed these "signs." This Greek word for "signs" (*sēmeion*) means a miracle designed to communicate a specific spiritual truth. A sign is a miracle with a message. It is a display of divine power that pictures an aspect of the salvation Jesus had come to give to humankind.

Nicodemus understood that the miracles performed by Jesus communicated a profound spiritual truth. He knew there was a deeper meaning behind them. But he did not discern what it was, and so he went to inquire of Jesus what the miracles meant. There was more to the miracles than met the eye—but what was their message?

Becoming a Miracle

The truth that Nicodemus needed to learn was quite simple. He needed to understand that he himself must become a living miracle. God must intervene in his life and exercise a display of divine power in his soul that would cause him to be born again. Nicodemus must experience this miracle. The power of God must be unleashed in his heart. He must become a new creation, something that only God could accomplish in his empty life.

The One speaking to Nicodemus was He who created everything out of nothing. John wrote earlier concerning Jesus, "All things came into being through Him, and apart from Him nothing came into being that has come into being" (John 1:3). This verse is a reference to Jesus Christ, who created everything that exists. Paul later wrote, "For by Him all things were created, both in the heavens and on earth, visible and invisible, whether thrones or dominions or rulers or authorities—all things have been created through Him and for Him" (Col. 1:16). This is the Creator who must create new life in Nicodemus. Jesus is the only One who could do so. John adds, "In Him was life, and the life was the Light of men" (John 1:4). Christ is life—He alone possesses life and gives life. The spiritual life that Nicodemus desperately needs can only come from Jesus. He has never been so close to the Giver of life, yet he was also so far away. Jesus must create this life within him.

A Work of Grace

This respected ruler possessed a spiritually dead soul that had been ruined by sin. His heart was filled with pride. His life was clothed with the filthy rags of his own self-righteousness. He needed cleansing in his inner being. Jesus must give him eyes to see this. This required that He infuse new spiritual life within him. Jesus must resurrect his spiritually dead soul and make him alive on the inside. Regeneration must do the inward work of creating new life in Nicodemus's barren soul. When Nicodemus came to Christ, he came as he was. But the new birth would not leave him there.

Nicodemus must be born again. The regenerating grace of God must give life to this spiritually empty man. He must be made into an entirely new person and given new life in order to see the truth and to discern the true nature of the kingdom of

God. The dead cannot create life. The new birth is something only God can do within him.

No Explanation but God

True believers in Jesus Christ have experienced this new birth from God. We know how someone can start over, because our old life has ceased to exist. We have received a new life that God has created within us. He gave us eyes to see the truth. We were divinely enabled to see who God is. We suddenly discerned why Jesus came. We grasped what His work upon the cross accomplished. We once were blind, but now we see.

Because we have been born again, we no longer serve ourselves. The glory of God now fuels our worship and stokes the flames of our desire for Him. We are energized to pursue the work that He has for us to do. Our life is a joyful offering to the One who birthed us into His kingdom.

The new birth dramatically changes us in every dimension of our life. It instills pride-crushing humility within us. It makes us call upon the name of the Lord. It causes us to give glory to God. Apart from being born again, we would be like spiritual corpses, ones with no spiritual life whatsoever and no recognition of God in our life. But by this miracle of grace, we are entirely new persons, dead to sin but alive to Christ.

Being born again does not mean a good person becomes better or a sick person becomes well. The new birth involves a far greater change than this. It is, more accurately, a dead person coming to life. It is like Lazarus being raised from the dead by Jesus. He was not merely diseased but deceased. He experienced a resurrection, not a resuscitation. He was lifeless and received new life in his dead body. This is precisely the radical transformation that occurs in the new birth.

Have You Started Over?

Starting over means admitting you have been wrong all your life. A new beginning means recognizing your life has been wasted. This requires renouncing every self-effort you have expended in order to commend yourself to God. It means acknowledging that every good deed you have offered to God is unable to raise you from the dead.

This necessitates denying yourself and humbling yourself before Jesus Christ. It requires that you believe in Him as your only hope of eternal life. You must cut out the things in your life that tempt you to sin and cause you to glory in yourself. You must repent of your sinful lifestyle and worldly lusts, turning 180 degrees to the opposite direction: pursuing the Lord Jesus Christ in obedience. Then, place your trust in Him entirely. He is worthy of your worship and praise, and joy will come as you make Him the whole crux of your life.

The old friends who used to give you worldly satisfaction are no longer your consummate joy. The old drinking or sexual habits are not your escape anymore. The job or relationships you relied upon to give you joy are no longer signposts of your identity. It is Christ alone who now consumes your interest and gives meaning to your otherwise empty life. He is the One who will help you to start over.

You must have a new heart for this new start.

eight

Soul Cleansing

Jesus answered, "Truly, truly, I say to you, unless one
is born of water and the Spirit he cannot enter into the
kingdom of God."

JOHN 3:5

The new birth does not simply repackage the exterior of our life. Merely restructuring the outside of our life but not changing on the inside is like putting a Band-Aid on terminal cancer. It would be like rearranging the deck furniture on a sinking ship. Such behavior modification would be only a superficial approach to the problem. What is needed to alter the interior of our souls is the work of God in regeneration. This divine activity operates on a far deeper level. The new birth makes us entirely new people from the inside out. It removes our old unbelieving heart and implants a new heart that believes.

But before God places a new heart within a person, He must cleanse the sin-stained soul. He will not place a clean heart inside a filthy soul. This internal cleansing is an important aspect of the work of God in the new birth. This divine act is portrayed as God pouring pure water on the soul and washing it clean.

This is what Jesus emphasized when He said to Nicodemus, "Truly, truly, I say to you, unless one is born of water and the Spirit he cannot enter into the kingdom of God" (John 3:5). What is the meaning of the water mentioned here? How are we to understand being "born of water"? Whatever its meaning, it is so important that Jesus began with the familiar phrase, "Truly, truly, I say to you," indicating Nicodemus cannot afford to miss the significance of what Jesus will say. What is its meaning?

Some take this water to refer to the release of fluid from the mother in childbirth. But this physiological reality is nowhere else mentioned in Scripture. That hardly seems the intent here. Others interpret this water as referring to water baptism. But Scripture never requires baptism for salvation. Jesus came to seek and to save the lost (Luke 19:10), yet He never baptized anyone (John 4:2). If water baptism was necessary for salvation, why did He never baptize? Still others understand this mention of water as a metaphorical reference to the word of God. Such is a possible interpretation here, but unlikely.

Cleansing of the Soul

Instead, this water is best understood to symbolize the inner cleansing of the soul in the new birth. This spiritual washing represents the internal purging of Nicodemus's inner life that would take place in the miracle of regeneration. In this passage,

Jesus used water as a synonym for the inner purifying work of the Holy Spirit. Our Lord will use two analogies in this dialogue for this inner ministry of the Spirit. One is water (John 3:5), and the other is wind (v. 8). Jesus uses these two word pictures to teach the truth of new birth.

These two metaphors for the Spirit—water and wind—picture the Holy Spirit as administering first a cleansing force like water and second an irresistible power like wind. Both characteristics of the Spirit work powerfully in the new birth. Wherever there is the one ministry of the Spirit, there will always be the other ministry.

At this point in the conversation, Jesus is stating that the Spirit's work purifies the sin-polluted soul like water. This is confirmed when Jesus later said to Nicodemus, "Are you the teacher of Israel and do not understand these things?" (v. 10). As *the* teacher in Israel, Nicodemus was well-taught in the Old Testament. He was the premier instructor of Scripture, well-studied in its teaching. He certainly possessed an extensive awareness of its many truths. Consequently, Nicodemus would have been thoroughly familiar with the significant Old Testament passages that teach the doctrine of regeneration. In these texts, the washing of water represents the Holy Spirit's work of regeneration. In the Old Testament, water often portrayed the ministry of the Spirit in purifying the sin-defiled soul. Nicodemus would have known this truth.

Sprinkled with Clean Water

In a previous chapter, we noted the key passage on regeneration in Ezekiel. It would be worth our while to revisit the truth of this text. Ezekiel prophesied during the Babylonian exile of the Israelites, due to their continued faithlessness and sin. He called the people to be reconciled to God by having their hearts washed clean. There, God spoke through the prophet, "I will sprinkle clean water on you, and you will be clean" (Ezek. 36:25).

In this pronouncement, God pledged to sprinkle cleansing water on sin-corrupted souls when He brings them into His kingdom. This is an exclusive work that God alone performs. When He says, "I will," He indicates the new birth is a singular effort on His part alone. It is not a joint effort by God *and* people. Instead, regeneration involves the sole activity of God alone. Only God can purify the human soul. This is a truth that Nicodemus should have known.

Washing Away Idolatry

This passage in Ezekiel further clarifies that God will cleanse us "from all your filthiness and from all your idols" (v. 25). This figurative language draws upon the old covenant practice of water purification. In Numbers 19:13 and 20, we learn that the priest threw water on persons or objects to symbolize the real cleansing needed. Sprinkling with water pictured the internal purification that accompanies the divine forgiveness of sin. Multiple Old Testament passages reference this divine pardon symbolized by water.

Under the old order, water was ceremonially sprinkled in the Levitical ritual of cleansing. Priests like Aaron, Moses's brother, would sprinkle lepers with water seven times for cleansing. Priests would also wash themselves before offering sacrifices at the altar. Numerous references for this are found in Exodus 30:19–20, Psalm 51:7, and Numbers 19:18.

Washing Away All Uncleanness

All this ceremonial sprinkling pictured the cleansing power of God in the hearts of people. This washing away of sin was also later mentioned in Zechariah 13:1. "In that day a fountain will be opened for the house of David and for the inhabitants of Jerusalem, for sin and for impurity." Here in Zechariah, God foretold that He would make sinners clean from their sin—through a greater descendant of David, Jesus Christ. Regeneration through the long-expected Messiah was figuratively described by washing with water.

As the leading teacher of Israel, Nicodemus would have been well-acquainted with these passages. Further, he should have known the most basic truth they represent. When Jesus explicitly said to him that he must be born of water, He meant it as a symbol of regeneration—this radical heart change—and the inner washing of the soul by the Spirit. In the new birth, the Lord sprinkles clean water upon filthy sinners and makes them clean. This is a spiritual cleansing that purifies us from the soul-damning defilement of sin. Such a washing permanently removes the indelible stain that exists within the human heart. Regeneration cleanses from sin by this inward purifying of the Holy Spirit.

Many scholars believe this verse could be translated, "Unless one is born of water, *even* the Spirit, one cannot enter into the kingdom of heaven." By this rendering, water and Spirit are used interchangeably. That is, the two mean the same. The mention of water simply illustrates the inward working of the Spirit. Just as the wind pictures the powerful movement of the Spirit (John 3:8), water represents His purifying effect (v. 5) by washing away the stain of sin and its judgment.

What comfort is brought to our heart when it is washed clean in the new birth! The haunting guilt of sin that condemns us is removed. Our defiled conscience is made pure. Our sin-stained soul is purged. A sense of peace fills our innermost being.

Washing Away Our Sins

This reference to water is what Paul meant when he gave his defense before the Jews in Jerusalem. In stating his testimony, the apostle said that God commanded him on the Damascus road, "Get up and be baptized, and wash away your sins, calling on His name" (Acts 22:16). Grammatically, the words "calling on His name" precede "Get up and be baptized." In other words, salvation is the direct result of calling upon the name of the Lord. The cleansing of sin immediately follows calling upon the Lord. It does not happen because of baptism. Paul makes that clear when he writes, "Whoever will call on the name of the Lord will be saved" (Rom. 10:13). No amount of water can wash away sin. Only the inner working of the Holy Spirit cleans the soul.

Paul affirms this same truth in his letter to the Ephesians. Here, he reinforces the washing of the soul in the new birth. "Christ also loved the church and gave Himself up for her, so that He might sanctify her, having cleansed her by the washing of water with the word" (Eph. 5:25–26). This means that Jesus washes and cleanses the church for whom He died by the inward ministry of the Spirit. The Holy Spirit works in tandem with the word of God to convict and regenerate the soul.

Washed in the Spirit

The apostle Paul elsewhere stressed this washing of water by the Holy Spirit: "Such were some of you; but you were washed, but you were sanctified, but you were justified in the name of the Lord Jesus Christ and in the Spirit of our God" (1 Cor. 6:11). In this verse, Paul refers to the spiritual cleansing by the Holy Spirit at the moment of regeneration. The haunting guilt of sin is purged from the convicted conscience. The condemnation of God that always accompanies sin is washed away. The believer is no longer enslaved to guilt and shame from sin but freed to obey God from the heart. This purifying from sin is symbolized in water baptism.

By way of historical background, the ancient city of Corinth was known for its gross sexual perversions and wickedness. Deep was the guilt of those who lived in this sin-infected city. There seemed to be no limits to the depths to which they had plunged into moral filth. However, Paul makes it clear that when one enters the kingdom, the Spirit cleanses the stained soul of its transgressions. No matter how great the sin in a person's life, the purging power of the Holy Spirit is far greater. The Spirit is able to wash away all guilt. There is no sin so great that the grace of God is not able to scrub it clean.

This washing by the Holy Spirit in the new birth is also highlighted in Paul's letter to Titus, which he wrote to help him combat false teaching that had seeped into the church in Crete. Paul describes the nature of true Christian living that flows from the new birth. "He saved us, not on the basis of deeds which we have done in righteousness, but according to His mercy, by the washing of regeneration and renewing by the Holy Spirit" (Titus 3:5). This is the inward cleansing of the soul in the new birth. The Agent of "regeneration" is the Holy Spirit, and the result is the "washing" of the human soul.

Every person has a conscience, which is a divinely given warning device. This internal alarm system bears witness to the soul of its condition. When we have sinned, our conscience accuses us. But the new birth cleanses the guilty conscience of wrong. The author of Hebrews explains, "Let us draw near with a sincere heart in full assurance of faith, having our hearts sprinkled clean from an evil conscience and our bodies washed with pure water" (Heb. 10:22). This washing by the Holy Spirit removes the inward sense of condemnation from the guilt-laden conscience. Those birthed into the kingdom are made pure. Subsequently, the outward act of baptism represents this inward reality that occurs in the new birth.

Cleansing the Guilty Conscience

This is precisely the same truth that the apostle Peter maintains: "Baptism now saves you—not the removal of dirt from the flesh, but an appeal to God for a good conscience—through the resurrection of Jesus Christ" (1 Pet. 3:21). This verse states that the water in baptism only symbolically pictures the cleansing of the guilty conscience. Peter was reminding the scattered first-century believers of the basis of their salvation being Christ. The new birth produces a good conscience. No amount of physical water can remove the spiritual pollution from the soul. It can only remove dirt from the body. This cleansing of the inner person can only be accomplished by regeneration.

When Jesus said, "Truly, truly, I say to you, unless one is born of water and the Spirit he cannot enter into the kingdom of God" (John 3:5), those words rang loudly in Nicodemus's ears.

This washing of water by the Spirit must take place within the sin-plagued soul of Nicodemus. His innermost being must be cleansed from the pollution of his own sin. He stands in dire need. He must have the stain of sin removed from his heart. The new birth is how God will cleanse Nicodemus, and God can wash him pure by the inner working of the Holy Spirit. The Spirit must apply the blood of Christ to remove his sin.

A Prime Example

Another man in the first century needed this same dramatic cleansing of his soul. He was a Pharisee like Nicodemus, and likewise was a ruler of the Jews in the Sanhedrin. He too knew the law inside and out. But this religious leader was far from wanting to come to Jesus to ask questions. In fact, he had an avowed hatred of Jesus Christ. This sin-hardened soul was so opposed to those who followed Jesus that he secured official papers to arrest them. He sought to drag them back to Jerusalem, where they would stand trial and suffer the death penalty.

This archenemy of Jesus Christ was Saul of Tarsus. He was a Pharisee of Pharisees, filled with an unholy zeal to persecute the early church. According to his own testimony, Saul was "circumcised the eighth day, of the nation of Israel, of the tribe of Benjamin, a Hebrew of Hebrews; as to the Law, a Pharisee; as to zeal, a persecutor of the church; as to the righteousness which is in the Law, found blameless" (Phil. 3:5–6). No one was a more devout Pharisee than Saul.

While Saul was traveling on the road to Damascus, a blazing light suddenly shone from heaven—the blinding glory of God. It knocked him off his high horse, throwing him onto the ground. This dramatic appearance was that of none other than Jesus Christ Himself. The Lord said, "Saul, Saul, why are you persecuting Me?" (Acts 9:4). In response to this confronting examination, he replied, "Who are You, Lord?" (v. 5). Saul answered his own question by the time he came to the end of the short sentence.

In that defining moment, Saul of Tarsus was born again. By a sudden work of grace, he was regenerated. Immediately, his old life passed away. A new life in Christ began. In that split second, this avowed enemy of the gospel changed his allegiance. He became a true follower of Jesus Christ. This professed foe was radically transformed. He became the apostle Paul—the chief proclaimer of the faith he once sought to destroy.

Drastically Changed Within

Not every new birth is as dramatic as a blazing light shining from heaven. But every divine act in regeneration is just as radical. The same new heart that was given to Saul is placed within all who are regenerated by the Holy Spirit. All who are born again are drastically altered in the depth of their soul— becoming an entirely new person in Jesus Christ.

If you are born again, this is what has transpired in your regenerated soul. God has drastically altered your soul, washed you clean, purged you from sin, and lifted you out of your guilt. You are not the same person you once were.

This Must Be You

If this miracle of the new birth has not taken place in your life, pray that it will. Ask God to open your eyes to your need for His grace. Seek the counsel of a mature believer to further explain the gospel to you. Search out the Scriptures to know more of who God is and what He has done in Jesus Christ to save sinners.

The cleansing power of the new birth can make even the greatest sinner pure before Him. In one moment, God can wash away an entire lifetime of sin. He can cause you to stand faultless before Him. His grace is all-sufficient to purge your soul of its guilty stains and clothe you with the perfect righteousness of His own Son, Jesus Christ.

Will you be made clean from your sins? Jesus has the power to wash you white as snow. Have you come to Christ for this inner washing by His grace? No one else can save you. Why would you wait any longer? Come to Him now in faith. Call upon His name. Commit your life to Christ.

nine

Spirit Born

That which is born of the flesh is flesh, and that which
is born of the Spirit is spirit.

JOHN 3:6

There is a fundamental principle of nature that like produces like. This unbreakable continuity is built into creation by the Creator Himself. An apple seed can only produce an apple tree, never a towering redwood. A watermelon
seed can only produce watermelon, never corn. An elephant
will never give birth to a baby eagle. Elephants reproduce elephants, and nothing else. It can never be otherwise, because
like produces like.

What is true in the natural world holds true in the spiritual
realm. When the Holy Spirit regenerates the human heart, He
reproduces a holy life in the soul. Nothing else can produce
spiritual life except the living God. When the living word is

planted like seed in the human soul, the Holy Spirit acts by the sovereign will of the Father and creates new life in the spiritually dead. This new life is spiritual life because it is created by the Holy Spirit. Like produces like.

A Continuity at Conception

This is precisely the truth that Jesus made clear to Nicodemus in John 3:6, distinguishing between two entirely different realms. The first is physical while the second is spiritual. Physical birth comes from a woman, giving birth to a new child. Spiritual birth comes from the Holy Spirit, giving birth to new life in a spiritually dead heart.

The flesh can only produce that which pertains to the flesh. Human nature can only beget human nature. Similarly, the Spirit will always produce a spiritual birth and can only produce that which belongs to the realm of the spirit.

The Flesh Produces Flesh

When Jesus said, "That which is born of the flesh is flesh," the term *flesh* refers to human nature. This word was also used earlier, in John 1:13–14. By "flesh," Jesus is referring to the human nature that everyone receives in their physical birth. To be born of the flesh is to have been conceived in your mother's womb. God alone creates physical life, as He works through the procreation of human parents. The result of this act is the creation of a human life that did not previously exist. After a new life is conceived in the womb, a woman carries a baby until she enters labor and gives birth to physical offspring. Flesh gives birth to flesh.

The Spirit-Generated Birth

Likewise, "that which is born of the Spirit is spirit" (3:6). It is the Holy Spirit who generates spiritual life in the heart. It is God's Spirit who produces a new nature, that is, a spirit nature that operates in the sphere of the kingdom of God. Jesus will later say, "God is spirit, and those who worship Him must worship in spirit and truth" (4:24). The fundamental principle is true of spiritual birth: like produces like.

If Nicodemus was to have eternal life, the Holy Spirit is the only One who could create it. No human being can bring spiritual life into existence. No human nature or human activity can effect this result. The new birth is exclusively God-generated, an inward work of the Spirit of God.

If you are born again, this is what God did within you. Regeneration dramatically transformed you at the deepest level. This change was from the inside out. You were immediately transferred from spiritual death to spiritual life. You suddenly passed from darkness to light. This change was so dramatic that you became a new creation. This God-given birth altered the fundamental nature of your mind, affections, and will.

A Comprehensive Birth

Years ago, a man walked into a church I pastored as the Sunday worship service began and sat down on the front pew. I had never met him, and he noticeably drew my attention. As I preached, he was visibly glued to every word I said. After the morning service was over, I spoke with him at the front of the church and asked if I could meet with him later that week. He agreed, and I will never forget that meeting.

As we visited over lunch, he began to pour out his heart. Though eminently successful in business and having the world in his pocket, he was empty on the inside. Moreover, he was under the deep conviction of his sin. He longed for a new start in life. He ached for a clean conscience before God.

I shared the gospel with him and the promise of God to give him a new heart. The news seemed to be too good to be true. I assured him that in the new birth, God gives a new heart in a clean soul. With tears streaming down his face, he bowed his head and committed his life to Jesus Christ—and his life was dramatically changed.

This man became a vivid example that the new birth is a comprehensive birth. A healthy baby is born into this world with all his or her body parts: two arms, two legs, and two eyes. These different body parts do not come in stages or over a period of time. A baby is not born with a set of legs but then later develops arms and, subsequently, feet. Neither is a baby born with one eye and five years later develops a second eye. To the contrary, every healthy baby arrives with all the needed body parts at the time of delivery.

The same is true when we are born again. In the new birth, God immediately works in the whole of our nature. Our minds are renewed. Our affections are reoriented. Our wills are redirected. It is not that our minds are changed but not our emotions and will. Rather, every aspect of our souls are reoriented toward God.

No part of our life remains unaltered by the rebirthing power of the Spirit. Our prior lusts no longer satisfy. Our desire for Christ eclipses our desire for endless entertainment. Our entire inner being comes under the sudden renovating work of God.

Head to toe, we are comprehensively born again. Everything is made entirely new by His divine power.

The Effects of Original Sin

This across-the-board change of nature in the new birth is necessary because of the wide-ranging effects of original sin. When Adam first sinned, the corruption of his offense was transmitted to the entire human race. With the conception of each person, the defilement of Adam's sin nature was passed down. No one escapes inheriting the total depravity of the fallen nature of the first human. No area of any individual's life is free from the all-pervasive depravity of sin.

This complete defilement of the whole human nature is what theologians call total depravity—that complete saturation of sin in the human heart, which we talked about in chapter 5. This truth does not mean that every person is as totally depraved as they could be. Not every person is a murderer or child predator. It does mean, though, that the depravity of Adam's sin has extended to the totality of every person's being. Every aspect of human nature has been corrupted by the deadly poison of sin.

As a result of original sin, sin darkens the *intellect* of every person. We live in spiritual darkness and cannot see the truth (1 Cor. 2:14). Likewise, sin defiles the *heart*. Everyone is born spiritually perverse and does not love God. Nor do we desire the things of His kingdom (Rom. 3:10–18). We love what we should hate and, conversely, hate what we should love. Moreover, the *will* is deadened by sin. We spiritually cannot choose what is right before God (John 6:44, 65). Consequently, every capacity—the mind, emotions, and will—of every person has been devastated by Adam's sin. Every part of every man and woman is polluted by sin.

The Reverse of the Curse

But there is hope. Regeneration is a comprehensive alteration of our whole person. The new birth produces an alteration at every level of our nature. Sin ruined every part of us, but the Spirit renews every part of our inner being. In the new birth, God reestablishes His reign in every region of our souls. The new birth is as wide-ranging in renewing our inner life as sin was in defacing it. Grace remodels the entire human soul.

Regeneration produces the change necessary to enter the kingdom of God. This inclusive transformation is all-encompassing. It is a holistic renovation of our souls by the Holy Spirit. The new birth alters our whole person with far-reaching change. This is the greatest change that could ever take place within our souls. This renovation comes from the new birth.

Hearing an Old Truth

When Nicodemus approached Jesus, he heard that he should have already known about this fundamental truth. As this conversation unfolds, Jesus will ask him, "Are you the teacher of Israel and do not understand these things?" (John 3:10). Clearly, Nicodemus *should* have known this truth. Jesus said so. In the Old Testament, God had already addressed the entire nature of the new birth. Through the prophet Ezekiel, God taught that this internal change of heart must come from Him. As previously noted, God declared, "I will give them one heart, and put a new spirit within them. And I will take the heart of stone out of their flesh and give them a heart of flesh" (Ezek. 11:19). He promises this inner change to those who approach Him by faith.

In this passage, God emphatically speaks of the fully integrated, thorough nature of the new birth. Only God, working by His Spirit, can execute this extraordinary claim. Mere religion cannot manufacture a new heart. No church can conceive this new life. No pastor or evangelist can do this. No Christian parent can transfer this to his or her child. God alone can give this new heart. The Creator alone can create new life in the soul.

Removing the Stony Heart

In this Ezekiel passage, God said, "I will take the heart of stone." A heart of stone is what the unregenerate person possesses and what we were born with when we entered this world. It is a heart that is hardened toward God, cold and without love for Him. It refuses to submit to the will of God. The stony heart refers to the unbeliever who is resistant toward God (2:7; 3:7). Such a stony heart is stubborn, self-willed, and indifferent toward the spiritual things of God. It is lifeless. A stony heart means the entire inner person is opposed to God.

This heart of stone must be removed before we can believe in Jesus Christ. Only the Great Physician can do this. He must take out the sin-hardened heart of stone. Such a heart is hard as a rock toward God. It is set against His truths in the Bible and rebels against His law. A hardened heart is unmoved by the gospel message. Though this heart may want the blessings God provides, it does not want God Himself. Those with such a heart only want to use God for their own selfish ends, for worldly things that He can give them. This is like a toxic relationship where a man only uses a woman for what she can give him physically. Such is selfish lust, not sacrificial love. Even so, the old heart merely desires to manipulate and use God, not love and serve Him.

Each of us must recognize our old heart for what it is. Even if we grew up in a church or a Christian home, we were still born with hard hearts of stone. This heart was hardened toward God and vile in His eyes. Loving God was impossible with our old heart of stone. We had a natural bent away from God. We were disposed toward disobedience. But in the new birth, God takes out this heart of stone and casts it away. This evil bias against God must be removed if we are to turn to Him.

Giving a Fleshly Heart

Considering this same Ezekiel passage, God pledged, "I will . . . give them a heart of flesh" (11:19). Whereas our old hearts were dead toward God, our new hearts are alive toward Him. They have a spiritual heartbeat for God and a strong pulse for His word. Our new hearts of flesh are responsive to the promises and commands of Scripture. These living hearts love God and prioritize the things of His kingdom. There could not be a more positive change in our life than this spiritual heart transplant.

Giving an Undivided Heart

In every true believer, the Lord has given a new heart. It is "one heart" (v. 19), meaning it is an undivided heart. It possesses one passion for God. This new heart does not have a divided loyalty. It does not split its allegiance between God and anyone or anything else. To the Hebrew mind, the heart represents all that a person is in their entire innermost being. Thus, when we are regenerated, all things become new. We are given a new mind to know God and new affections to love Him. He grants us a new will to obey Him. Our new heart has new desires, new ambitions, new hungers, and new thirsts. This divine gift makes us, and everything about us, new.

Giving a United Heart

In this same passage in Ezekiel, God says, "I will . . . put a new spirit within them" (v. 19). When God regenerates us, He implants a new spirit within us. This new spirit refers to the new governing power of our mind. It directs our thoughts and guides our perspectives. In the new birth, God implants new attitudes, new priorities, new inclinations, and new desires within our soul. Our mindsets are entirely altered. God reverses our affections. Our intentions are dramatically rerouted. He gives us a new will with new loyalties and new allegiances. God makes us new from the tops of our heads to the bottoms of our feet. We each become a new creature in Christ Jesus.

A teacher with such strong credentials as Nicodemus would surely have known these words from Ezekiel. He should have known all about the new birth, though it was taught by this heart transplant analogy. But he missed it. He should have known that this new spirit could be received only through the new birth. There it was in the Bible, clear as a bell, recorded by the prophet. But Nicodemus could not grasp it.

In past ministry, I have encountered others, many of them church members, who, try as they might, could not grasp this heavenly truth. They were loyal in their church attendance, seemingly present every time the church doors were open. They were involved in ministry, serving with much energy. But their eyes were closed to their need for the new birth. They presumed that they knew God, when, in fact, they did not. Until God gives sight to spiritually blind eyes, they cannot see the truth.

Giving a Spirit-Indwelt Heart

In the new birth, the Lord also places the Holy Spirit into our souls. God promises to place the Holy Spirit within us when He brings us into His kingdom. When He regenerates us, He also comes to indwell us. Thus, God Himself comes to abide within us when we are birthed by His Spirit. We become the holy temple where the living Spirit abides.

Because of His indwelling presence, our new lives in Christ are lived in the all-sufficient power of God. The same Spirit who convicts us also calls us and is conforming us into the image of Christ. The Spirit causes us to desire and pursue personal holiness on a daily basis. We are not merely made alive but then left to live the Christian life on our own. To the contrary, God gives us His Spirit to supernaturally enable us to function in this new life with Him. Without His regenerating grace, we would be unable to live as God intends us to live.

Giving an Obedient Heart

When God places His Spirit within us, He redirects our will to follow His will. God's word tells us, "I will put My Spirit within you and cause you to walk in My statutes, and you will be careful to observe My ordinances" (Ezek. 36:27). Our old lives of disobedience are redirected by the Spirit toward faithful obedience to God's word. The divine law that we once disregarded will now be kept from the heart. It is only with this new heart of flesh that we can obey and follow Christ.

In this divine act of regeneration, the Spirit gives us new desires to keep His commands from a new heart of love for God. When we are born again by the Spirit, we begin to live to honor God. We are given new desires to live in humble compliance to His statutes. As soon as this new life is imparted to us, a new walk with the Lord begins in pursuit of holiness.

An Exclusive Work of God

It is important to note once again that this new birth is exclusively a saving work performed by God alone. God gives us this new heart at a time when our old hearts are hardened against Him. Rather than striking us dead, which we deserve, God makes us alive. While we are still resisting Him, God reaches down and does what only He can do in us.

When God puts His Spirit within us, He causes us to begin to walk in His commandments. The Spirit of truth produces a new desire for obedience to the word. He begins to lead us down a new path marked by personal purity. The moment He regenerates us, we immediately begin to observe His ordinances. Granted, our complete perfection will never be realized in this life. Nevertheless, the desire to live without sin will be present within us. New life patterns begin to develop within us. Old practices of sin suddenly pass away. A new compliance to the word characterizes our life when we are born from above.

Let me be clear: our obedience does not produce the new birth. Rather, it is the new life from God that causes this obedience. This new life of obedience is like the growing features of a newborn baby: the birth necessarily leads to the continued growth. Wherever there is regeneration, there will be spiritual growth in sanctification. A new heart will always produce a new lifestyle of obedience to God.

Years ago, I knew a man who, like Nicodemus, by all outward appearances was a highly moral man. He served in leadership in our church and had gained the respect of all. But unknown to us—and to him—he had not been born again. As he sat under the preaching of the word of God, it soon became clear to him that he was an unregenerate person. As he could not point to evidences of the new birth in his life, he came to the sobering conviction that he was lost and perishing.

As the seed of the word was being sown into his heart, God caused that seed to germinate and produce new life in Christ. This successful but empty man was born again. The change that God effected in him was noticeable by all. He suddenly was possessed with new love for God.

If this change of heart has not yet occurred within you, ask God to cause you to be born again. Only God can do this within you. You must experience this divine birth in which God creates new life in your dead soul. No greater change could ever happen in you. When God takes out your heart of stone and gives you a heart of flesh, all things will be made new. You will never be the same again. Such an alteration is a comprehensive change of your entire inner being. It is the total renovation of your soul from the inside out. By this divinely wrought miracle, you will become a new creature in Christ Jesus.

What about You?

Has this comprehensive change occurred in your life? Have you felt these longings for God and new desires for holiness within you? Do you witness this new obedience to the word? If not, humble yourself before God. Ask Him for this new heart. This is a prayer that He delights to answer.

If He has changed your heart, rejoice and give Him praise. Join a local church and befriend an older Christian to guide you in your new Christian growth. Spend as much time as you can communing with God—grow your relationship with Him through reading His inspired word and praying to Him. He will keep you and grow you—through eternity.

ten

Divine Mandate

Do not be amazed that I said to you, "You must be born again."

JOHN 3:7

E ntering the kingdom of God is not a complicated matter involving multiple checkpoints. It does not require navigating a confusing maze of blind turns. There are not blind steps that a person must follow to enter the kingdom of heaven. There is only one necessary step that lies ahead. To enter the kingdom of God, a person simply must be born again and believe in Jesus Christ. This is the one non-negotiable.

As Jesus said to Nicodemus, "You must be born again" (v. 7), the same is true for you and me. All that is required to become a child of God is quite simple. We must be born a second time. To enter this world, we were born physically. Nothing else. That singular step was the sole prerequisite. In like manner, all that is necessary to enter the spiritual realm of salvation is to be born again. Nothing else is required.

You Must Be Born Again

This was the clear message Jesus delivered to Nicodemus when this religious leader approached him. As this dialogue unfolded, the Lord stressed, "Do not be amazed that I said to you, 'You must be born again'" (John 3:7). This leading figure in Israel must not be surprised by the necessity of the new birth. He was no different from anyone else. Human nature is all the same. The need for salvation that applied to anyone else also applied to Nicodemus.

Nevertheless, Nicodemus was clearly "amazed" by this mandatory requirement made by Jesus. The word "amazed" (*thaumazō*) means "to wonder, to marvel, to be astonished." This non-negotiable bewildered this religious leader. What Jesus mandated visibly shook him. Could this demand be true?

Do You Mean *Me*?

Nicodemus responded, "How can these things be?" (v. 9). Was he not living a morally pure life? So it seemed. Had he not done more good works than his peers? Had he not faithfully attended the worship services in the temple? Had he not been fully involved in serving the Lord? Was he not the leading Bible teacher? Surely he was better than others. How could Jesus say this to *him*?

Nicodemus was completely caught off guard. This was the total opposite of what he expected to hear. He probably thought he would be given the assurance of his salvation. As he processed this pronouncement by Jesus, he was left utterly speech-less. Never had Nicodemus heard an assessment of his life like this.

Many who do not know Christ feel the same way. When you believe yourself to be a moral, upright person, you are shocked to hear you are headed for hell. It seems impossible to be facing divine judgment when you are a self-prescribed "good person." Using earthly scales of justice, you are not quite as bad as *that* person over there. How can you believe you desperately need regeneration when you see your acts of community service and kindness as earning you a place in heaven?

The Divine *Must*

Jesus now reaffirms what He said earlier concerning the neces-sity of the new birth. But this time He uses even stronger words. Rather than toning down this mandate, He intensifies it. "You must be born again" (v. 7). The word *must* stresses the obligatory nature of being born again. Jesus underscores how mandatory the requirement of the new birth is to enter the kingdom of heaven. There is no entrance into the realm of salvation apart from it. Nicodemus could not adopt a "take it or leave it" atti-tude regarding this requirement. There is no other path or point of access into the kingdom. He must be born again.

There is no other door by which the highly moral person may enter. The same new birth must take place in our life no matter who we are—whether we are a criminal or a church member. Every person must come to this same place. We must see ourselves as helpless sinners in desperate need of the new birth. Moreover, we must do more than recognize it—we must experience its reality.

Why is the new birth absolutely necessary for entrance into the kingdom of God? Why is being born again non-negotiable? It is crucial to consider the answers to these important questions.

Defiled Hearts Cannot Enter

First, the new birth is absolutely necessary because a person living outside the kingdom of God is morally defiled, being inwardly polluted by sin. No one can enter the kingdom until he or she is cleansed within. As we saw previously, this is why Jesus said to Nicodemus that he must be "born of water and the Spirit" (v. 5). As discussed earlier, water is a symbol that describes the cleansing of the soul by the Spirit in the new birth. Water is a picture of the inward washing that occurs in regeneration. Only this divine flood can purge the soul of its indelible stain of sin.

Nicodemus *must* be born again because his soul is defiled by sin. We know this is true because Nicodemus, like all people, has sinned and falls short of the glory of God (Rom. 3:23). The Bible says, "There is none righteous, not even one" (v. 10). This defilement includes Nicodemus. He is sinful and separated from a holy God. He cannot come to God as he is. God is too holy, and Nicodemus is too sinful—an enormous chasm separates the two. This, however, is a sobering realization to which he had not yet arrived.

God Is Absolutely Holy

The truth of the holiness of God makes the new birth an absolute necessity. In Isaiah 6, the prophet Isaiah has a vision of God's majestic holiness. He witnesses the seraphim around the throne of God, crying out day and night, "Holy, Holy, Holy, is the LORD of hosts, the whole earth is full of His glory" (Isa. 6:3). Isaiah's response can only be, "Woe is me, for I am ruined! Because I am a man of unclean lips, and I live among a people of unclean lips; for my eyes have seen the King, the LORD of hosts" (v. 5). When someone catches a glimpse of God's holy glory, the only right response is deep conviction of one's sin, as Isaiah experienced.

The word "holy" (*qadosh*, Hebrew) has a twofold meaning. It comes from a root word that means "a separation." The idea is to cut an object into two pieces so that the two halves can be separated from each other. Thus, the holiness of God separates Him from His fallen creation.

This primary meaning of the holiness of God signifies that He is high and lifted up, seated in the heavens, exalted above creation in His ruling power. This truth reveals that God is lofty and transcendent, majestic in regal glory, dazzling in the splendor of His awesomeness. He is separated from sinful humankind. Consequently, God "dwells in unapproachable light, whom no man has seen or can see" (1 Tim. 6:16). The blazing holiness of God is blinding to the eyes of sinful humanity. A broad divide separates holy God from fallen people.

God's Moral Perfection

The secondary meaning of divine holiness deals with God's moral perfection. That is, God is absolutely blameless in His own character. He is flawless in all His ways, sinless, without any taint of imperfection. The Bible says, "God is Light, and in Him there is no darkness at all" (1 John 1:5). In other words, there is no dark side of God. There are no moral blemishes in Him. Every aspect of His divine nature is perfectly pure.

As a result, no sinful human can enter the holy presence of God in their fallen state. In the book of Habakkuk, the prophet wrestles with God about the realities of Judah's judgment. As Habakkuk acknowledges God's character, he says, "Your eyes are too pure to approve evil. And You can not look on wickedness with favor" (Hab. 1:13). This means that the holy eyes of God cannot look upon any sinner with His acceptance. Every sinful person is condemned because of the depravity of his or her wickedness.

The Washing of Water

For any morally flawed creature to enter the presence of a holy God, we must first be born again. It is by the washing of regeneration that defiled humans are made pure in the sight of God. The new birth is necessary for any sinful person to be made acceptable before God. Only those who are made clean by the Holy Spirit can be found admissible in the sight of God.

This is why Jesus said to Nicodemus that he *must* be born again. Mere religion cannot wash away the moral defilement that has stained his soul. No amount of good works can purge his heart of the pollution within. To be made suitable before God, he must be born of water. That is, he must be born of the Spirit.

Blind Eyes Cannot See

Second, the new birth is also necessary because the spiritually blind cannot see the kingdom of God. This is the requirement

Jesus made earlier: "Unless one is born again he cannot see the kingdom of God" (John 3:3). The word "see" (*eidon*) means "to see with understanding." The idea is to see the truths of the kingdom of God with perception or discernment. In other words, we must be born again before we can truly perceive the things of the heavenly kingdom. All unconverted individuals are spiritually blind and incapable of comprehending gospel truths. They cannot grasp how these truths relate to their lives.

Concerning this spiritual blindness, Paul writes that "the god of this world has blinded the minds of the unbelieving so that they might not see the light of the gospel of the glory of Christ" (2 Cor. 4:4). The devil darkens the understanding of unbelievers so they cannot see their need for the gospel and blinds the eyes of all who are in an unregenerate state. He causes a black shroud to cover their spiritual eyes. The evil one makes the allure of the world seem more appealing than the truth of the gospel. With their minds darkened, they are unable to see their way to enter the kingdom. As a result, they refuse the light of truth and reject the gospel. "For even though they knew God, they did not honor Him as God or give thanks, but they became futile in their speculations, and their foolish heart was darkened" (Rom. 1:21).

The new birth is necessary because it gives spiritual sight to those who are blind and live in darkness. No one can believe in Jesus Christ until they can behold Him for who He is as Savior and Lord. God must give spiritual eyes first before anyone can enter the kingdom.

Jesus will later heal a blind man, giving him sight (John 9:1–41). The Lord made clay and applied it to his eyes. He then told the man to wash in the pool of Siloam. The pool of Siloam was a source of fresh water in Jerusalem, and poor and sick people often used it to bathe. When the blind man did as Jesus instructed him, his sight was restored. This miracle created quite a controversy with the Pharisees. Jesus used this miracle as an object lesson to show what the new birth is like. It is an act of divine grace that gives spiritual sight to those blinded by their sin. Jesus said that He came "so that those who do not see may see" (v. 39). This reference is to sight being given to the spiritually blind, and this healing also showed that the Pharisees remained blind and in darkness.

Nicodemus was one of these blind Pharisees. He lived in a world of spiritual darkness and could not see the most basic spiritual truths concerning entrance into the kingdom of God. Though he had studied Scripture his whole life, he could not behold the poverty of his spiritual bankruptcy. Neither could he grasp the divine operation in the new birth. The Spirit must open his eyes, or he will never enter the kingdom.

Stubborn Wills Cannot Submit

Third, the new birth is necessary because persons outside the kingdom of God are stubborn and will not submit to the authority of God. Like rebellious children, they simply will not humble themselves to respond to the free offer of the gospel. Their hearts are defiant and unwilling to humble themselves before Christ in meekness. They are stiff-necked in their resistance to the gospel, as their hearts are hardened in unbelief.

But in the new birth, a hardened heart is replaced with a softened heart that loves Jesus Christ. This new, pliable heart loves what it previously hated—the Lord—and it hates what it previously loved—sin. A spiritually stiff-necked heart is replaced with a submissive heart that yields to the lordship of

Christ. A spiritually obstinate heart is made tender to the things of God and receptive to receive the truth.

In the new birth, defiant sinners are made humble by grace. Previously proud persons are brought low before God. Self-autonomy is removed. Self-determination becomes a thing of the past. Self-obsession vanishes. These old things have passed away. In their place, a lowly submission before God comes. A new humility fills the heart. No one struts into the kingdom. The new birth crushes such arrogant pride. Humility floods the soul. A new Master rules the heart.

Dead Souls Cannot Believe

Fourth, the new birth is necessary because any person outside the kingdom of God is a spiritual corpse and cannot believe in Christ. Unregenerate souls are "dead in [their] trespasses and sins" (Eph. 2:1). They are "dead in [their] transgressions" (Col. 2:13). Being spiritually dead, they are utterly incapable of taking the determinative step of faith to enter the realm of salvation. Dead people cannot come to Christ by faith. They are without life and cannot believe the gospel. A spiritually dead individual has no moral ability by which he or she can repent. Such a person is incapable of responding to gospel truth. To believe the gospel, we must first be spiritually resurrected to life.

Apart from being born again, no one has any capacity to believe in Jesus Christ. Those who are dead in sin remain unresponsive to spiritual truth when it is presented to us. God must regenerate us before we can exercise saving faith. The new birth gives us the spiritual capacity to respond to the gospel. It is the new birth that produces a living faith in Christ.

The regeneration of the soul gives new life to a new heart. This impartation of spiritual life enables those previously dead in sin to believe in Christ. In that moment, the new birth gives listening ears to hear the call of the gospel. It gives active feet to run to Christ. It gives receptive hands to embrace Him by faith. The new birth gives a liberated will, released from its bondage to sin, to believe in Jesus Christ. Not until a person is made alive in the new birth can he or she enter the kingdom of God.

A Non-Negotiable Necessity

Is it any wonder that Jesus stressed to Nicodemus that he *must* be born again? Given the stronghold that sin has in his life, it is apparent why Jesus maintained that he must be born again. Apart from the new birth, Nicodemus cannot enter the kingdom of God. No matter how religious he was, how much of the Bible he knew, or how rigorous his spiritual disciplines were, if he was to see or enter the kingdom of God, he *must* be born again. There would be no special exemption granted to him from this one necessary thing.

What Jesus said to Nicodemus, He says to each one of us. If we are to enter the kingdom of God, we too *must* be born again. Down through the centuries, this single requirement remains a timeless non-negotiable. What was true two thousand years ago remains just as true at this moment: we must be born again.

Do Not Be Amazed

Does this necessity of the new birth amaze you as it did Nicodemus so long ago? Are you astonished that the Lord would say this to you? Are you staggered by this stipulation? Does what Jesus says shock you?

Maybe you think this new birth is not necessary because you see yourself as a morally good person. Perhaps you have grown up in a religious family. Possibly you were married in a church. Maybe you have given your time and resources to help others.

But God says your works can contribute nothing to your new birth. "For by grace you have been saved through faith; and that not of yourselves, it is the gift of God; not as a result of works, so that no one may boast" (Eph. 2:8–9). Your religious affiliation will never put you in a right standing with God. Jesus emphasizes the necessity of this true transformation to you—just as He did to Nicodemus.

eleven

Irresistible Power

The wind blows where it wishes and you hear the sound
of it, but do not know where it comes from and where it
is going; so is everyone who is born of the Spirit.

JOHN 3:8

The greatest miracle that God ever performs is the new birth. Greater than when Jesus turned water into wine two thousand years ago is when He transforms a polluted heart into one that is spiritually pure. Greater than when He opened blind eyes at the pool of Bethesda is when He gives spiritual sight to see the glorious light of the gospel. Greater than when Jesus raised Lazarus from the dead is when He resurrects a soul and grants eternal life.

The greatest demonstration of the power of God is in the new birth. The power God displays in the spiritual realm is always greater than what He does in the physical world. Greater than when God spoke all creation into being is when He makes a person to be a new creation. Greater than when God said, "Let there be light," is when He shines spiritual light into a sin-darkened soul. Greater than when He made the realm of nature is when He creates a new nature within us. Greater than when God creates new life in the womb is when He creates new life in the heart. What God does in the spiritual realm is always His greatest work.

A Bedrock Truth

This truth of the powerful activity of God in the new birth came through loud and clear as Jesus addressed Nicodemus. In this ongoing conversation, Jesus added, "The wind blows where it wishes and you hear the sound of it, but do not know where it comes from and where it is going; so is everyone who is born of the Spirit" (John 3:8). By these words, Jesus wanted this religious leader to know that his regeneration was entirely out of his hands. His new birth was completely dependent upon the will of God. If Nicodemus was to be born again, it would not be by his own choice. It would be decided by the perfect will of God.

Jesus taught this truth about the independent prerogative of God by using the analogy of the wind. In fact, the word for "spirit" (*pneuma*) is the very same word for "wind" in the Greek language. An intentional parallel is communicated by this metaphor. How the wind operates in the physical realm is how the Holy Spirit works in the spiritual realm.

What exactly does Jesus intend to teach by this comparison? In this chapter, we will focus on four important aspects of how the movement of the wind illustrates the operation of the Spirit in the new birth. Through these four truths, we will discover that the Holy Spirit works independent of persons according to His own will.

Only God Sends the Wind

First, Jesus begins by stating that the movement of the wind cannot be directed by anyone. Jesus said, "The wind blows where it wishes." Independent from our control, the wind has a mind of its own. It blows wherever God desires it to blow. The wind does not move at our bidding. It blows exclusively by divine initiative. No human being has the slightest influence over the direction of the wind. No human can steer its movement. God alone guides the path of the wind.

To support this truism, the Bible says, "God caused a wind to pass over the earth" (Gen. 8:1). The wind goes exactly where God sends it. When the weather forecasters say that a hurricane in the Atlantic Ocean is going to make landfall at a particular location, it will inevitably shift its course and move elsewhere. This is because the wind follows its own path. The wind does not consult us. The wind cannot be directed in any particular direction. We cannot accurately predict the path of the wind, much less control it. God alone is the One who directs the wind.

So it is with the working of the Holy Spirit in the new birth. The Spirit moves as He is directed by the eternal will of God the Father. The Spirit blows into the lives of those chosen by God for salvation. The path that the Spirit takes is according to the sovereign will of the Father. The Spirit moves where God sends Him to regenerate spiritually dead souls. This chosen path is completely independent of our will. No person holds the reins of the Spirit or can regulate His activity. The new birth occurs by the independent movement of the Spirit.

No One Can Stop the Wind

Second, Jesus taught that the wind is irresistible. When it moves across the surface of the earth, it cannot be hindered by humankind. In its full strength, the wind overpowers whatever lies in its path. In the midst of a hurricane, massive trees are blown over. Houses are relocated. Buildings are leveled. Cars are toppled. When a tornado strikes, it cuts a swath through an entire community, leaving destruction in its path. Such a formidable force subdues everything in its way. The wind is unstoppable, as everything yields to its movement.

The parallel that Jesus is making is obvious. The Spirit is irresistible in His omnipotent movement to cause the new birth. The will of God is far greater than the will of humankind. The Spirit shatters human pride. He conquers our resistance and overcomes all human excuses that have long refused Christ. When the Spirit blows, He sweeps away all preconceived prejudices against the gospel. He humbles once-stubborn hearts. The Spirit softens hardened wills to believe in Christ.

Wherever the Holy Spirit unleashes His power in regeneration, He removes all obstacles that would block His entrance into a life. When the Spirit blows, human hearts surrender to the lordship of Christ. The Spirit makes the unwilling heart to be willing in the day of His power.

Such was the case when Paul preached the gospel in Philippi. As the apostle proclaimed the truth there, a woman named Lydia, who was from Thyatira, was listening. Though she was a worshiper of God in some general sense, her heart remained closed to the gospel. But as the apostle preached the message of salvation, the Bible says, "the Lord opened her heart to respond to the things spoken by Paul" (Acts 16:14). Though her heart had been barred shut her entire life, this time it was different.

As the gospel was preached by Paul, the Spirit threw open the closed doors of her soul. The truth of the saving message entered triumphantly and won her heart to faith in Christ. Her life was dramatically changed. Lydia became a new person in Christ. Afterward, she insisted that Paul and his companions stay with her family. The new love shown in her hospitality was a result of the miraculous change in her heart.

The Wind Is Invisible

Third, Jesus explained that the wind cannot be seen by the human eye. No one can see the wind when it blows, because it is invisible to the naked eye. But anyone can certainly feel its dominant force when it moves through the air. Though we cannot see the wind, we can be easily overpowered by it. We can be moved by the wind when it blows. We can see its obvious effects. The fury of its movement can strike a sense of awe in our heart.

The same is true with the movement of the Holy Spirit in the new birth. No one can actually see the Holy Spirit in His life-giving operations of regeneration. The Spirit does not have a corporal body that the human eye can see. He cannot be observed by the naked eye. But we can certainly see the powerful effects of His working. We can see His effects; we can feel His conviction and the fear of God He produces. Though the Spirit is invisible, His activity in our hearts is, nevertheless, unmistakable.

Consider your own life before you were converted to Christ. You had repeatedly resisted the truth of the gospel. For years, you had refused to believe in Jesus Christ and enter the kingdom. But one day, you unexpectedly responded in a different way.

You suddenly felt your dire need for the saving mercy of God. Your proud heart was humbled. You were made receptive to the truth of the gospel. Why was your response different this time?

The answer lies not with you. You had not become a better person, enabling you to believe. You had not become smarter overnight. The difference in your response can be attributed to God alone. Unseen to your physical eye, the invisible hand of God was powerfully at work within your soul. The Spirit blew into your life and took away every excuse you had long offered. The Spirit brought you to the end of yourself. You were born again. Though you had not previously believed, you suddenly confessed your sin and put your trust in Christ. Saving faith was birthed in your heart by the life-giving Spirit.

When Peter preached on the day of Pentecost, many previously hardened hearts were suddenly convicted of their sin. Only weeks earlier, they had been a part of the mob that cried out for the crucifixion of Christ. But now they were cut to the core of their being. They cried out, "What shall we do?" (Acts 2:37). Peter replied, "Repent," and three thousand souls were saved. What made the difference? The answer lies with God the Holy Spirit. Under His convicting power, they were born again.

This is what God did in your life as one who has been regenerated by the Spirit. Where you once refused the gospel, you were made to believe in Jesus Christ. This was the work of the Spirit, convicting you of sin and opening your heart to put your trust in Jesus Christ.

The Unknown Direction

Fourth, Jesus stated that the blowing of the wind is incomprehensible. In this analogy, the route the wind takes defies human explanation and its path far exceeds a person's ability to accurately predict. Meteorologists have long demonstrated their inability to explain exactly where and when the wind will blow. So often, a storm blows in the opposite direction than was forecast. In this sense, the movement of the wind is mysterious. Its path is unpredictable. It defies explanation.

For example, in 1943 the Texas coast was threatened with an approaching storm. Within a couple days, this tropical storm grew in intensity to become a full-powered hurricane. With winds up to 132 mph, the hurricane destroyed buildings, homes, and churches. Its path could not be deterred, directed, or detained. Houston residents could not predict the path of the wind.

So it is with the movement of the Holy Spirit in the new birth. The direction the Spirit moves cannot be predicted. The person whom we think is most likely to be converted is often not. At the same time, the individual whom we think will never believe often does. Such are the inscrutable ways of God in the new birth. When the Spirit blows, He often chooses the most unlikely path. He often works where we least expect and when we least anticipate among people we would not imagine.

Simply put, the path that the Holy Spirit takes is unfathomable. None of us can know upon whom He will operate next. Solomon acknowledges this inexplicable mystery. "Just as you do not know the path of the wind and how bones are formed in the womb of the pregnant woman, so you do not know the activity of God who makes all things" (Eccles. 11:5). Known to God alone is how and when He will work to create a physical conception in the womb. The same mystery holds true in a spiritual conception that produces the new birth in the heart.

The prophet Isaiah also recognizes the imponderable ways of the Holy Spirit. In speaking to Israel during a time of judgment, Isaiah provides the people with reminders of comfort and hope. While outlining the majesty of God's character, Isaiah writes, "Who has directed the Spirit of the LORD, or as His counselor has informed Him? With whom did He consult and who gave Him understanding?" (Isa. 40:13–14). The meaning of these two rhetorical questions is clear. The Holy Spirit travels a path that escapes human reason, but He always operates with perfect wisdom.

The apostle Paul acknowledges the same when he writes: "Oh, the depth of the riches both of the wisdom and knowledge of God! How unsearchable are His judgments and unfathomable His ways! For who has known the mind of the Lord, or who became His counselor?" (Rom. 11:33–34). The answer to these probing questions is so obvious that the apostle does not need to answer them. No one knows the chosen path of God in salvation. His ways in regeneration are beyond our calculation.

Because we know God is worthy to be trusted, we can rest in the choices of His sovereign will. Knowing His ways are perfect, we can continue praying for unsaved family members. Although we will never understand Him fully, we know His choices are always directed by His great love. His transcendent ways are revealed in who He causes to be born again.

Two Sides of the Same Coin

As we noted in the first chapter, the apostle John teaches two sides of the same coin with regeneration and conversion: "But as many as received Him, to them He gave the right to become

children of God, even to those who believe in His name, who
were born, not of blood nor of the will of the flesh nor of the
will of man, but of God" (John 1:12–13). John first describes
the *effect* of the new birth, then its *cause*. The effect of the new
birth is that we receive Christ into our life by faith. But how is
it that we believe in Him?

The first three assertions in this verse are negative, explain-
ing how we are *not* born into the kingdom of heaven. We are
born again "not of blood nor of the will of the flesh nor of the
will of man" (v. 13). The fourth statement is positive, teaching how we *are* reborn. This is important enough to review
more fully.

Not Inherited by Human Descent

The first negative denial states that we are born again "not of
blood." In other words, the new birth has nothing to do with our
physical birth or family lineage. The fact that our parents may
be Christians does not automatically mean we are regenerated.
Growing up in a Christian home does not make us born again.
God has no spiritual grandchildren. We must have new life in
Christ that comes independent of our bloodline, and it is made
real only by being regenerated by the Holy Spirit.

Not Achieved by Human Efforts

The second negative denial that John makes is that we are born
again "not of the will of the flesh." This means that our regeneration is not the result of our own moral efforts or our religious works. Through our own efforts, we could never reach
the necessary standard of perfection that is required to enter

the kingdom. We could never be godly enough to conceive the new birth in our heart.

Another key passage that makes this crystal clear was written by the apostle Paul: "He saved us, not on the basis of deeds which we have done in righteousness, but according to His mercy, by the washing of regeneration and renewing by the Holy Spirit" (Titus 3:5). Paul concurs with the apostle John, that regeneration is not by our deeds of righteousness. That is, it is not by our donations to charity or our kind actions to strangers. Instead, it is strictly by the unmerited mercy of God.

Not Initiated by Human Choice

The third negative denial is that we are born again "not of the will of man." This is an important designation, because when we are unsaved, our will toward God is spiritually dead and unable to respond to any presentation of the truth. When we are "dead," we do not have a free will toward Christ. Such ability is nonexistent. When we lay in the grave of our sin, our will is held in bondage to our sin and rendered inoperative toward God. We possess the power of choice in only one direction: namely, toward sin and transgression.

This important truth is known as the bondage of the will. It teaches that before we are born again our will is held enslaved by our old master, sin. We are fastened in chains to the devil and the kingdom of darkness. We love the darkness rather than the light and have no appetite for what is right. We possess no power of choice toward a new master, Jesus Christ. The Spirit has to liberate us from our chains of sin before we can believe the gospel.

But Realized by Divine Operation

Since our new birth is not caused by anything in us, it must be entirely by God. John succinctly asserts that the new birth is "of God" (John 1:13). Regeneration is accomplished solely by the powerful operation of God in our heart. He alone wills and works within us in the new birth. We receive Jesus Christ because God first created divine life within us. This work of grace enables us to come to faith in Christ. A fundamental principle of theology is that God is always before everything else. He exists previously, before all things. Nowhere is this truer than in our new birth.

The apostle Peter teaches that God alone accomplishes the work of regeneration in each of us. He writes, "Blessed be the God and Father of our Lord Jesus Christ, who according to His great mercy has caused us to be born again to a living hope through the resurrection of Jesus Christ from the dead" (1 Pet. 1:3). This means that our new birth is singularly caused by the sovereign activity of God. He alone causes us to be born again. Therefore, He deserves all the praise for our new life in Christ.

Elsewhere in the Bible, the will of God is again represented as the sole agent in our new birth: "In the exercise of His will He brought us forth by the word of truth, so that we would be a kind of first fruits among His creatures" (James 1:18). This verse leaves no room for any doubt but that the will of God exclusively accomplishes our new birth. God alone is the author of our regeneration, as He works through the instrument of His word.

Emboldening Our Witness

God's sovereignty in salvation should be a strong encouragement to us when witnessing to others who do not know Christ.

Though they are hardened to the gospel, the most resistant heart can be quickly softened by the Spirit. Even in the face of their opposition, we should never give up hope in speaking to them about Christ. No matter how apparent their rejection of the gospel may be, we should continue to pray for unconverted people and share the gospel with them. The working of the Spirit cannot be resisted when He exerts His might.

Like the force of hurricane winds, the effect of the Spirit can overpower the resistance of any person. I have lived in what is known as Hurricane Alley, where powerful winds can blow in from the Gulf of Mexico. When these winds make landfall, they exceed 100 miles per hour. They often flatten whatever is in their path. Trees are pushed over like toothpicks. Cars are tossed around like tumbleweeds. Everything yields to the force of the hurricane winds. So it is with the movement of the almighty Holy Spirit. Hearts are blown open, and unbelief is removed. Saving faith is swept into the soul under its sway.

Consequently, we should not worry about our inadequacies in sharing the gospel. We can trust God that, as we speak the truth, the Spirit will do His work that is necessary to bring about their new birth. This truth should embolden our witness for Jesus Christ. We can tell others about the grace of God and faithfully spread the message of the gospel far and wide. The doctrine of regeneration gives great freedom to witness for Christ, knowing that He will save those He has chosen.

Jesus's command to "Go therefore and make disciples of all the nations" (Matt. 28:19) is mandatory. Our calling is to advance into the world with the saving message of Jesus Christ.

So we can be emboldened, knowing the gospel is "the power of God for salvation to everyone who believes" (Rom. 1:16). Know that the Spirit will overcome all resistance in those whom God has chosen. When the Spirit moves, He cannot be hindered.

twelve

Enduring Truth

Nicodemus said to Him, "How can these things be?"
Jesus answered and said to him, "Are you the teacher
of Israel and do not understand these things?"

JOHN 3:9-10

S ome truths are so clearly taught in the Bible that everyone who reads them should innately know what they mean and their relevance for their lives. Not every truth, though, rises to this same level of clarity. Admittedly, some teachings are easier to grasp than others. But the truth and necessity of the new birth is presented in Scripture in such a lucid manner that it should be known by all.

What Jesus discussed with Nicodemus is a biblical truth that He expected him to know. The teaching on regeneration was so elementary that Jesus fully expected this noted teacher to know this fundamental doctrine. Jesus unequivocally stated that, as the primary teacher of Israel, Nicodemus should have a sound grasp on this truth. He should know about the necessary work of the Spirit in performing a spiritual heart transplant. This core teaching had already been expounded throughout the Old Testament. Was not this the book that Nicodemus had supposedly mastered?

A State of Confusion

In this dramatic encounter, Nicodemus said to Jesus, "How can these things be?" (v. 9). By such a perplexed response, this religious leader was obviously stunned to hear what Jesus stated about his need for the new birth. "These things" refers to the nature of the Spirit's work. Nicodemus was asking, "How can God be in complete control of my gaining eternal life?" This ruler of the Jews was accustomed to thinking that *he* was in control of his relationship with God. But now Jesus has informed him of the very opposite. The Lord asserted that the Holy Spirit had absolute authority over his relationship with God.

How can these things be?

Sarah responded in a similar way when she overheard a mysterious visitor saying to Abraham, "Your wife will have a son" (Gen. 18:10). Laughing in disbelief, Sarah recognized she was far past the age of childbearing. The heavenly visitor responded to her incredulity with the rhetorical question, "Is anything too difficult for the LORD?" (v. 14). Just as God had to miraculously create life in the barren womb of Sarah, God must also create new life in the dead heart of Nicodemus.

How can these things be?

Mary asked the same question. When told by an angel that she would bear a son, she asked with incredulity, "How can

150

this be, since I am a virgin?" (Luke 1:34). She was stunned that she would give birth to the promised Messiah. Recognizing the utter power and sovereignty of God in her circumstances, Mary acknowledged her submission. "Behold, the bondslave of the Lord; may it be done to me according to your word" (v. 38).

This is how Nicodemus should have responded to this mandate by Jesus that he be born again. But due to the stubbornness of his unbelieving heart, Nicodemus refuses to believe the necessity that he be born again. He rejects Christ's words.

How can these things be?

Nicodemus was stunned to learn that, in his present condition, he could not see the kingdom of heaven—and in fact must start over with God. He has just heard that his spiritual life has been a total waste to this point. All his good works have not contributed anything toward entering the kingdom of God. All of his religious efforts have not brought him any closer to heaven. All of his Bible knowledge has not gained him any access to God.

If that were not enough, Nicodemus also learned that his soul must be washed clean by the Holy Spirit. He was like a dirty object in need of cleansing in order to be acceptable to God. He, a Pharisee—one who has separated himself from all that is unclean—was inwardly defiled. He was just like everyone else: in need of a new heart.

What is more, Nicodemus was told that the Spirit works in human hearts wherever He chooses to work. He had no control over the saving activities of God. He was entirely at the mercy of God.

The Perceived Foolishness

Nicodemus could not grasp these most basic truths because he had not been born again. He could not see with spiritual understanding these simple truths about the kingdom of God. Paul explains this spiritual blindness when he writes, "But a natural man does not accept the things of the Spirit of God, for they are foolishness to him; and he cannot understand them, because they are spiritually appraised" (1 Cor. 2:14). In other words, "natural" people are those who have had only a natural birth and remain in their fleshly state. Consequently, they cannot comprehend the spiritual message that is being presented or grasp this teaching about a supernatural birth. When they hear this truth, it sounds like sheer foolishness. They cannot perceive how it relates to their lives.

This is precisely where Nicodemus found himself. He was a natural man struggling to discern the truths of another realm, that of a supernatural world. He was like a blind man trying to appreciate a beautiful painting by Rembrandt. Nicodemus simply did not have the spiritual capacity to hear or see the truths of the kingdom of God. Thus, he was completely perplexed by what Jesus said to him.

How can these things be?

Nicodemus believed he had to work for his salvation. He was convinced he had to be better than others to enter the kingdom. In fact, he actually believed he *was* better than others. What he could not accept was the fact that he needed to be born again. Further, he could not accept that his spiritual birth was out of his hands. Nicodemus could not let go of his legalistic, works-oriented system of human achievement to gain salvation. The truth of grace was a foreign language to him.

You Still Do Not Understand?

In response, "Jesus answered and said to him, 'Are you the teacher of Israel and do not understand these things?'" (John 3:10). This rhetorical question clearly implies that given his lofty position as the premier Bible teacher in the nation, he should know these truths. This lack of understanding is inexcusable. A recognized teacher of Nicodemus's stature, with his considerable exposure to the Old Testament, would be expected to know these things. Jesus was holding him responsible to grasp the truths of the new birth as they are plainly taught in the Scriptures.

So, where in the Old Testament is the truth of the new birth presented? What passages in the law should have flashed to the forefront of Nicodemus's mind? What words of the prophets should have leaped off the page and captured his attention? A brief survey of these verses will be helpful to our understanding.

The Circumcision of the Heart

The first mention in the Old Testament of teaching on the new birth is the spiritual circumcision of the heart. Circumcision was the prescribed practice of cutting the male foreskin on the eighth day after birth. It carried a national significance, symbolizing that Israel had been set apart by God for His saving purposes on the earth. But this rite also brought with it an individual significance. It pictured that each heart must be pierced by the Spirit and set apart by God for Himself. This fundamental truth is taught in many passages in the Old Testament, which Nicodemus should have known.

A circumcised heart is a Spirit-regenerated heart that produces love for God. When Moses spoke to the nation of Israel before they were to enter the promised land, he declared vitally important truths from God. After forty years of wandering in the desert, the people were ready to enter the very place where God intended them to represent Him before the other nations. The people stood on the plains of Moab, poised and ready to enter the land of their future home. But before they could enter, their hearts had to be made right with God. This holy mission required holy hearts.

In light of this, Moses announced, "The LORD your God will circumcise your heart . . . to love the LORD your God with all your heart and with all your soul, so that you may live" (Deut. 30:6). For Israel, this spiritual circumcision was crucial to set them apart from the pagan nations around them. Moses said it was a divine act that must cut the human heart. The result of this spiritual surgery is loving God with our whole being. We, in turn, live. The obvious implication is that before this divine procedure, the uncircumcised heart does not love God. Neither does this heart know life but rather is spiritually dead.

The Heart Must Be Pierced

God required the circumcision of the heart in order to have a new start with Him. The Abrahamic covenant established the rite of circumcision (Gen. 17:10–14) in which God said the administration of this procedure would be a sign of his covenant with Abraham. This rite was later reaffirmed in the Mosaic covenant (Lev. 12:3). Circumcision was a badge of Jewish identity, a sign of belonging to the covenant community. The elders administered this rite to Jewish boys on the eighth day after their birth. The cutting of the foreskin symbolized that the nation of

Israel had been chosen by God to be His own possession. God set apart his people for His purposes.

However, a circumcised Jewish boy still needed to have his heart circumcised by God. Physical circumcision was only the outward sign of the inward reality that must take place within the heart and soul. This spiritual cutting by the invisible hand of God would provide the painful conviction of sin that would yield devotion to Him.

Spiritual Surgery Needed

Spiritual surgery must be performed by the invisible hand of God within a person. The heart must be set apart to God. The religious rite of circumcision pictured the reality of the new birth. The physical practice merely signified the spiritual act of being cut off from one's old life of sin. This spiritual operation by God produced a heart consecrated unto a new life of loving allegiance to Him.

The Lord promised He would circumcise the hearts of His people. Without this surgical procedure in the inner person, no individual can enter God's kingdom. Salvation becomes real only when God pierces the heart. The soul must come under the divine knife. He must cut open the heart and perform His regenerating work. God does this when His Spirit pierces the heart, using the sharp, two-edged sword of His word.

From Generation to Generation

In speaking to Israel before they entered the promised land, Moses addressed their future as a nation. He maintained that God would circumcise "the heart of your descendants" (Deut.

30:6). In other words, this would be an ongoing, saving work by God that He would perform into the future. Their offspring would need more than a physical circumcision in order to enter His kingdom. Their descendants would also need a spiritual circumcision as much as the present generation did. If their children and their children's children were to enter the realm of salvation, they must be spiritually circumcised. Throughout the centuries, this internal procedure was a necessary work that God must perform in the soul. This necessity was true in Moses's day, continued to Nicodemus's day—and it continues to this present hour. This work of grace would later become identified by Jesus as the new birth.

Each individual in every generation must have this spiritual surgery performed upon their heart. We are not automatically born into a state of grace by virtue of family background or religious heritage. Everyone born into this world must be spiritually circumcised if they are to receive eternal life. This spiritual circumcision causes us to "love the LORD your God with all your heart and with all your soul, so that you may live" (v. 6). This surgery performed by God's invisible hands implants a new love for God in the sinner's dead heart that previously did not exist. Whenever God circumcises the heart, it produces new affection for God. There is a new devotion to His word and a new allegiance to God. This new heart is aligned with God. It loves what God loves and hates what He hates. This divine operation brings about a dramatic change in the core of our innermost being.

Circumcised, Yet Uncircumcised

The prophet Jeremiah also stressed this need for a spiritual circumcision of the heart. He prophesied during a difficult time in

Judah's history, with much surrounding political and spiritual turmoil. In the midst of this calamity, Jeremiah proclaimed the spiritual solution to their national problems. By way of background, the people of God had been engrossed in the sin of flagrant idolatry for forty years (Jer. 2). The people were sacrificing their children to the god Molech outside of Jerusalem. This also involved worship of "the queen of heaven" (7:18; 44:19). Surrounding this idol worship was their own hypocrisy toward God, which bred adultery and injustice against the defenseless.

To right these wrongs, the prophet asserts, "'Behold, the days are coming,' declares the LORD, 'that I will punish all who are circumcised and yet uncircumcised'" (9:25). At first glance, these words appear to be contradictory. How can a person be circumcised and yet be uncircumcised? It seems that it should be one or the other. How can it be both?

The simple explanation is that there are two different kinds of circumcision being addressed. One is a physical circumcision and the other is a spiritual one. The physical circumcision is performed on the body, while the spiritual one is in the soul. The external circumcision is a ritual administered as a symbol. But the internal circumcision is the reality the sign symbolized. With this distinction, there were many in Israel who were physically circumcised yet spiritually uncircumcised. Countless numbers had received the physical sign but not the spiritual reality. The true circumcision is the spiritual circumcision, which is necessary to enter the kingdom of God.

The prophet then states, "All the nations are uncircumcised, and all the house of Israel are uncircumcised of heart" (v. 26). Here he acknowledges that the unbelieving foreign nations are "uncircumcised." But so also, "all the house of Israel are uncircumcised of heart." The clear implication is that many in Israel were surgically cut in their flesh, but their hearts remained un-regenerate. God had never pierced their hardened hearts with His word and had never given them spiritual life. Though they were citizens of the nation, they remained outside the kingdom of God. This is a careful distinction that must be stressed.

What God Will Do

In further prophecies of Jeremiah, the truth of regeneration is presented with even greater clarity.

> "Behold, days are coming," declares the LORD, "when I will make a new covenant with the house of Israel and with the house of Judah, not like the covenant which I made with their fathers in the day I took them by the hand to bring them out of the land of Egypt, My covenant which they broke, although I was a husband to them," declares the LORD. "But this is the covenant which I will make with the house of Israel after those days," declares the LORD, "I will put My law within them and on their heart I will write it; and I will be their God, and they shall be My people. They will not teach again, each man his neighbor and each man his brother, saying, 'Know the LORD,' for they will all know Me, from the least of them to the greatest of them," declares the LORD, "for I will forgive their iniquity, and their sin I will remember no more." (Jer. 31:31–34)

In this pronouncement of "I will," God asserts six times what He will do in the human heart. This divine work is independent of any effort by humankind. We do not read God saying, "*you* will," as though we are the physicians of our own souls. Neither do we read God saying, "*we* will," as though this heart surgery is a joint effort between God and us. Instead, this passage records that God announced, "*I* will," stressing His sole activity in the new birth. God *alone* will put His law within us and write it upon our heart. He *alone* will forgive sin. He *alone* causes obedience from the heart. If 99 percent of our salvation depended on God and only 1 percent of our salvation depended on us, we would fail every time. Being born again is completely out of our control and entirely in the hands of God.

There is great application of this truth to the heart of every Christian. The fact that the new birth is entirely a work of God brings a great assurance of salvation. As we experience a new desire to obey the word of God, we can know this is evidence that God is at work in our heart. Such desires are produced exclusively by God in our new heart. Countless other passages in the Bible confirm this, not the least being, "By this we know that we have come to know Him, if we keep His commandments" (1 John 2:3). Simply put, obedience brings assurance that God has implanted a new heart in the new birth.

Implanted in the Heart

In this internal working, God said, "I will put My law within them" (Jer. 31:33). The divine word will no longer be an external part of the Israelites' lives. The truth of Scripture will no longer simply lay on the surface. The word will now be implanted in the depths of their hearts, the epicenter of their being. The Bible later states that one must "receive the word implanted, which is able to save your souls" (James 1:21). This engrafting enables us to receive the word that will save our souls. Like seed sown into the soil, the word of God must be planted by Him into the heart (1 Pet. 1:23). Then He must cause it to germinate and spring forth with life.

In this prophecy, God further states, "On their heart I will write it" (Jer. 31:33). This divine promise pledges an inner working that is even deeper than the previous one mentioned: He will write His word on their hearts. God will not write His words on stones as he did at Mount Sinai with the Ten Commandments. In this divine act, He will inscribe it upon tablets of human flesh, giving personal knowledge of God through His word. They will not merely have the truth in their heads, but it will be engraved upon their hearts. By this work of grace, the word of God will take root in their hearts and grow, bearing much fruit.

When the word of God is written on our hearts, it remains indelibly etched within those who are born again. Once written there by the divine hand, it will remain permanently. What God has written, no one can blot out.

A Heart-to-Heart Relationship

In this same divine promise, God announced, "I will be their God, and they shall be My people" (v. 33). He will enter a personal relationship with those whose hearts He opens and will bring them into His kingdom. He will personally care for them. He will provide for and protect them. He will guide and direct them. In reality, God will be to them everything they need. By this divine intervention, He promises an intimate, close relationship with them.

This heart-to-heart relationship is true for all believers in every generation. If you are a believer in Jesus Christ, this is true in your life too. As you walk through life, God will be with you every step of the way. He promises His presence with you: "I am with you always, even to the end of the age" (Matt. 28:20).

Likewise, He promises His provision for you: "And my God will supply all your needs according to His riches in glory in Christ Jesus" (Phil. 4:19). Moreover, He promises His personal and fatherly care for every trial of your life: "After you have suffered for a little while, the God of all grace, who called you to His eternal glory in Christ, will Himself perfect, confirm, strengthen and establish you" (1 Pet. 5:10).

As this prophecy continues, God develops this truth of the new birth yet further. "They will not teach again, each man his neighbor and each man his brother, saying, 'Know the LORD,' for they will all know Me, from the least of them to the greatest of them" (Jer. 31:34). Each person in whom God works His miracle of regeneration will have equal access to Him. They will have the same close proximity to Him as anyone else. No matter their background or social standing, every believer shares the same access to and intimacy with God. There will not be a hierarchical structure within His kingdom. All regenerated souls will have the same experiential knowledge of God. Thus, no one will need to teach them about God, because each one will know Him intimately and personally.

God Will Forgive Their Sin

Finally, God concludes, "I will forgive their iniquity, and their sin I will remember no more" (v. 34). Those whom He births into His kingdom will be those whose iniquity will be forgiven. Personal sin has placed each person in infinite debt to God. Years of disobedience and rebellion have accrued a debt impossible to repay. When Jesus died, He "canceled out the certificate of debt consisting of decrees against us, which was hostile to us; and He has taken it out of the way, having nailed it to the cross" (Col. 2:14). That is, the Israelites' debt incurred against God will be canceled. Their offense will be pardoned.

In the new birth, God will cancel out their transgressions based upon the long-awaited death of a future sacrifice, the sinless substitute, Jesus Christ. It will be on the basis of His atoning death that God will forgive their iniquities. God states, "Their sin I will remember no more" (Jer. 31:34). God will no longer hold their sins against them. Their forgiveness is as complete as if the offense against God never occurred. They have been permanently freed from any condemnation (Rom. 8:1).

He Should Have Known

On the basis of these Old Testament passages, Nicodemus should have known about his own need for a new, circumcised heart. He should have read that God must write His word upon his heart and do an internal work of grace within it. But tragically, he remained in the darkness about this fact.

Nicodemus should have also known what the prophet Ezekiel wrote. In earlier chapters, we noted that God must perform a heart transplant within him (Ezek. 11:19; 36:25–27). God must take out his heart of stone and implant a heart of flesh inside him. This is the heart transplant that Nicodemus needed.

A Sobering Reminder

Nicodemus stands as the primary example of someone who can know much about the Bible but never receive its truths into his heart. He is a model of one who knows much Scripture in his head but does not know God in his heart. Here is a man who knew countless facts from the word of God but had no personal knowledge of its Author.

Do not let this be true in your life. Do not trust in your family's heritage of faith. Do not look to your church attendance to place you in the kingdom. Do not be like Nicodemus, who trusted in his religious activity to gain him a new heart. No matter how much you may know *about* the Bible, you must know God Himself. And there is only one way to know God—by the new birth.

thirteen

Unbelief Confronted

Truly, truly, I say to you, we speak of what we know
and testify of what we have seen, and you do not accept
our testimony. If I told you earthly things and you do
not believe, how will you believe if I tell you heavenly
things? No one has ascended into heaven, but He who
descended from heaven: the Son of Man.

JOHN 3:11–13

P eople who read the Bible the most can often know it the least. Ironically, the more they know its facts, the less they know its message. They have accumulated much information about Scripture but lack the illumination to understand what it means for their lives. They know many details about the word of God but cannot discern how it applies to them. They have amassed a wealth of Bible knowledge but lack the faith to assimilate it into their lives. The more they learn, the less they live it.

This may describe where you once were. Maybe you were raised in a Christian home and grew up involved in church. Maybe you attended a Christian school. If so, you had a great advantage of exposure to the truths of the Bible. But though you may have learned much about the Bible, you remain outside the kingdom of God until you are born again.

This was the case with Nicodemus. He knew much about the Bible. In fact, he knew more than anyone else in the nation. He could quote specific sections of Scripture and give the rabbinical interpretation. However, though he knew the letter of the law, he did not know the spirit of it. Though he instructed others, he himself had not been taught by God. Despite his vast knowledge of Scripture, he remained ignorant of what was required of him to enter the kingdom. Sure, he knew *about* God. But He remained a distant stranger to Nicodemus.

When Christ declared that Nicodemus stood outside the kingdom, this respected religious leader was dazed. When Jesus explained to him the nature of the new birth, he should have already known about it. After all, the truth of regeneration in the heart was a basic teaching in the Old Testament. Jesus boldly asserted that Nicodemus should have read Scripture more carefully. This Pharisee had completely missed one of the most essential truths in the entire Bible. The necessity of the new birth still remained a mystery to him.

A Faulty Foundation

As we discussed earlier, Nicodemus confidently presumed that his sterling reputation, impressive knowledge, and religious heritage would commend him to God. But he could not have been more wrong. Can you relate? Was there a time in your past when you were convinced you were right in spiritual matters with God but were really dead wrong? There are many things we can risk being wrong about, but we cannot risk being wrong about the state of our soul with God.

We can know truths about God, quote Bible verses, and know the ins and outs of systematic theology. But if we have not been born again—if our desires have not been changed to embrace Christ by faith—we are as lost as the staunchest atheist down the street. It is crucial to have a new heart from God if we are to truly know Him for who He is and to worship Him as the Lord of our life. Only when we can humble ourselves before Him, confess our complete dependence on His grace, repent, and believe in Him can we truly know Him.

The Problem of Unbelief

As this dialogue with Nicodemus unfolded, Jesus put His finger on the live nerve in this proud Pharisee's soul. Jesus said, "Truly, truly, I say to you, we speak of what we know and testify of what we have seen, and you do not accept our testimony" (John 3:11). Nicodemus's problem was not that he suffered from a lack of knowledge about the Bible. Instead, Nicodemus suffered from a failure to *believe* what was written in the Bible.

This direct challenge by Jesus once again begins with the familiar phrase "Truly, truly, I say to you," which signals the extreme importance of what Jesus will say immediately following these words. What He is about to say will rise to the highest level of critical importance. With these words Jesus intended to capture Nicodemus's attention so he would not miss the full impact of what He is saying. As Jesus often described the crowds who listened to Him, so it was with Nicodemus. He "had ears to hear, but did not hear." Jesus used this phrase to refer to people who were spiritually stubborn and not receptive to the truths He spoke.

Such unbelief in Scripture long plagued the entire nation of Israel. Like hyper-religious people in our day, the Jews knew the minutia of the Bible but not its essential message. They missed seeing the way of salvation altogether. Jesus would soon indict the Pharisees, saying that they "strain out a gnat and swallow a camel" (Matt. 23:24). In other words, these highly religious people focused upon the details but missed the meaning. They majored on minor points and minored on major points. Consequently, they remained in unbelief concerning the most important part of the Bible. Jesus would also say, "You search the Scriptures because you think that in them you have eternal life; it is these that testify about Me" (John 5:39). They were oblivious to the way of entrance into the kingdom.

As a result, Jesus said, the Pharisees "shut off the kingdom of heaven from people" (Matt. 23:13). Furthermore, Jesus charged, they "[did] not enter in" themselves. Despite having Scripture, they remained in unbelief. This included Nicodemus, who had not yet entered the kingdom of heaven.

One Voice, One Message, One Way

Jesus said to Nicodemus, "We speak of what we know and testify of what we have seen" (John 3:11). To understand this, it is important first to identify to whom Jesus is referring. By this plural pronoun "we," Jesus is identifying Himself with many others who have testified to Nicodemus concerning the truth. These multiple witnesses include the whole testimony of what the Old Testament prophets preached and wrote. These human mouthpieces for God included men like Moses, who led God's people through the wilderness; Isaiah, who prophesied about the fall of Jerusalem; and Micah, who predicted both the judgment and restoration of God's people. Also included is the preaching of John the Baptist, as well as what Jesus Himself taught. All these God-sent messengers spoke with one voice concerning the way of salvation. There was no contradiction between their testimonies. Together, they testified the same message concerning the way into the kingdom.

What Jesus said to Nicodemus is perfectly consistent with the message of all the prophets who had come before Him. This truth about the necessity of the new birth was not a new requirement for entering the kingdom of God and did not reveal a newly conceived route to salvation.

Of all the important truths about salvation, this is the most important one that Jesus is stressing. There was not one way of entering the kingdom of God in the Old Testament and an entirely different one in the ministry of Jesus. There was not one way for a Jew to be saved but a different way for a gentile to be reconciled to God. No matter who a person is, whether a leading teacher of Israel or an uncircumcised gentile, there is only one way to find admission into the kingdom of heaven. In the message of salvation, there is an unbroken continuity from the Old Testament prophets, to John the Baptist, to Jesus Christ Himself. The apostles will maintain this same consistency throughout the New Testament. The only way to God is through the new birth.

Anytime, anywhere, anyone has ever been made right with God, it has always been by the inner working of the Holy Spirit, who gives faith in Jesus Christ. Those who believed this message in Old Testament times were saved by looking *ahead* to the coming of Jesus and His atoning work. Similarly, those in Jesus's day were saved by looking *to* Him. In like manner, those who believed after Jesus's ascension to heaven are saved by looking *back* at His first coming and His work upon the cross. From the first book in the Bible, Genesis, to its last book, Revelation, this is the only gospel message. This seminal truth had not yet transformed Nicodemus.

The Heart of the Issue

Jesus now addressed the heart of the problem with Nicodemus. He said, "And you do not accept our testimony" (v. 11). "You" is plural and represents the nation of Israel, blinded by its works-righteousness religion. Jesus was saying to Nicodemus that he and the entire nation had chosen not to accept the clear testimony of the Old Testament. They would not receive the message of John the Baptist, nor would they believe the words of Jesus. The heart of Nicodemus's problem was the same: he failed to believe the testimony of these God-sent messengers, including the message of the new birth.

When Jesus used the word "accept" (*lambanō*)—"you do not accept our testimony"—it means "to take by the hand, to lay hold of." This is precisely what Nicodemus failed to do with the gospel witness given throughout the Old Testament. The heart of the issue was the issue of his heart. He failed to lay hold of the biblical testimony that had been made known to him. Along with the vast majority of Israel, he was blinded by his self-righteousness and consequently refused to receive the message of salvation by faith. Simply put, he rejected the good news that had been delivered to him through the many Old Testament writers.

Later in this same discourse, Jesus said to Nicodemus, "He who does not believe has been judged already, because he has not believed in the name of the only begotten Son of God" (v. 18). The one who does not believe is already under the judgment of God. John the Baptist will add that, for the one who does not obey the gospel with saving faith, "the wrath of God abides on him" (v. 36). His solemn words emphasize that unbelief results in divine wrath.

The Sin of Unbelief

What began as a two-way dialogue between Nicodemus and Jesus was now becoming a one-way discourse by Jesus. From this point forward, Jesus would be the sole speaker. He said, "If I told you earthly things and you do not believe, how will you believe if I tell you heavenly things?" (v. 12). By saying, "you do not believe" (v. 12), the Lord passed the divine judgment that Nicodemus was an unbeliever. He has not accepted the truth of the gospel. Nicodemus had not humbled himself and admitted his need nor repented and confessed his sins. He did not believe the message of the prophets. He did not receive the testimony of Christ. Instead, he believed in himself.

Nicodemus chose to remain entrenched in his legalistic approach to salvation. He chose to continue to look to himself to merit his acceptance before God. He chose the sin of unbelief, leaving him spiritually lost. This is what unbelief does. It defiantly refuses to believe the free offer of the gospel. It rejects the assessment of Christ concerning what its true need is. It denies Jesus the place of preeminence in a person's life.

Instead of turning to lesser things to be our identity—financial prosperity, relational security, or even good works—we must turn to Christ by faith. Instead of resisting His call to surrender our life to Him, we must submit to and chase after Him. Repenting from a lifestyle full of empty pursuits, vain joys, and delight in sin, we can instead delight in the Triune God. If we remain in legalism or loose living, we will surely perish in our sins.

> Take care, brethren, that there not be in any one of you an evil, unbelieving heart that falls away from the living God. But encourage one another day after day, as long as it is still called "Today," so that none of you will be hardened by the deceitfulness of sin. For we have become partakers of Christ, if we hold fast the beginning of our assurance firm until the end, while it is said,
>
> > "Today if you hear His voice,
> > Do not harden your hearts, as when they provoked Me." (Heb. 3:12–15)

From the Simpler Truths

By saying, "If I told you earthly things and you do not believe, how will you believe if I tell you heavenly things?" (v. 12), Jesus makes a clear distinction between two different levels of truth. "Earthly things" refers to the basic truth conveyed by the "earthly" analogy of the new birth, and "heavenly things," means the profounder truths of heaven above, where God dwells. This would include the relationship between the Father and the Son (John 1:1, 18), as well as between the Father, the Son, and the Spirit (1:32–33; 3:8). The Father, Son, and Holy Spirit have been in perfect and intimate communion with one another throughout eternity past. The truths of this trinitarian relationship are lofty, complex, and mysterious. "Heavenly things" also include other matters pertaining to the eternal counsel of God, such as sovereign election (1:13) and effectual calling (6:44). These truths display God's choosing authority, electing some to salvation and drawing those people to Himself through His grace.

Jesus reasoned with Nicodemus that if he could not understand these simpler truths about the new birth, how would he possibly understand profounder truths? In other words, first things first. Nicodemus must first apprehend the basic doctrines of salvation before he can grasp more complex teachings. This simpler truth begins with understanding the plain teaching about the new birth and his need for regeneration.

Nicodemus cannot teach others the way into the kingdom until he himself has entered into it. He cannot teach others until he has been taught by God. He cannot impart to others what he does not possess. He cannot take others where he himself has not gone.

Truth from Above

Further expounding this principle about saving faith, Jesus adds, "No one has ascended into heaven, but He who has descended from heaven: the Son of Man" (3:13). This is to say, no one has ascended into heaven to learn more about God and then returned to earth to tell what he or she has learned. However, there is One who has descended from heaven to come to this earth so that He may tell us about God. This person is the One addressing Nicodemus: the Son of Man, Jesus Christ. If Nicodemus is to know the way to heaven, he must listen to Jesus, who came down from heaven to speak to him.

Jesus is the One who truly knows the Father. He said, "No one knows the Son except the Father; nor does anyone know the Father except the Son" (Matt. 11:27). Jesus came down from heaven to reveal Him to men. The Son of God (John 3:16, 18) became the Son of Man (v. 14) in His incarnation, to enter this world and explain the Father to humankind (1:18). The revelation of the invisible God through Jesus Christ was so crystal clear that He later said, "He who has seen Me has seen the Father" (14:9). Jesus's words to Nicodemus must be received as being from the One who has descended from heaven to earth to bring this message about how to enter the kingdom. But if Nicodemus did not accept even the "earthly things" concerning the new birth, he would certainly not be able to receive "heavenly things" of a more profound nature.

Standing at the Crossroads

Nicodemus found himself standing at the crossroads of life. Never had the truth been more clearly presented to him than at this moment. Never had the way of salvation been so openly taught to him than in this personal encounter with Jesus. The deep questions with which he had been wrestling have been directly addressed. Nicodemus must make a decision. Would he believe what Jesus said about the new birth?

Jesus pressed Nicodemus at this very point. He must decide how to respond to this teaching. Would he continue in his self-righteousness or humbly ask God to birth him into His kingdom? Nicodemus must answer. Divine truth is never intended to be merely learned and known. It must be acted upon. Truth always demands our response. So, would Nicodemus believe the truth spoken by Jesus? Or would he continue in his unbelief?

Which Way Will You Go?

For many of you holding this book, you stand at the very same intersection of life. There are two paths before you: one path is the way of self-righteousness, and it leads to eternal destruction. The other path is the new birth, and it leads to eternal life. You must decide which way you will travel. The truth has been clearly presented to you. You must receive this divine testimony concerning your personal need for the new birth. To die in unbelief will cause you to appear at the final judgment without an Advocate and Savior. This truth is perfectly consistent with the testimony given by the prophets in the Old Testament. The entire Bible is speaking to you with one clarion voice. It declares that you must be born again and believe in Jesus Christ.

If you have never believed in Jesus Christ, the words that He spoke to Nicodemus so long ago are calling you to commit your life to Him. Repentance is a renunciation of all confidence in yourself to commend you to God. It is the denial of your self-efforts in order to trust Jesus Christ with your life and eternal destiny. As you would take food or drink into your body for life, saving faith is receiving Christ as Lord and Savior for true life.

Act now, without delay. This is the most important decision you will ever make.

fourteen

Saving Faith

As Moses lifted up the serpent in the wilderness, even
so must the Son of Man be lifted up; so that whoever
believes will in Him have eternal life.

JOHN 3:14–15

The greatest evangelist who ever lived was Jesus Christ. He
was, unquestionably, the most gifted winner of souls who
ever gave witness to the gospel. He was the most effective fisher of men to those perishing in the vast ocean of their
sins. He was the greatest harvester in fields already white unto
harvest. Many have preached the gospel to more people. Others have seen more individuals brought into the kingdom. But
none ever proclaimed the gospel more effectively, with greater
precision, than Christ did.

Whenever Jesus presented the truth, He relentlessly moved
His presentation of the gospel to the decisive point where He

would call individuals to believe in Him. So it was in this exchange with Nicodemus. Jesus brought this discussion about the new birth to a bottom-line decision: Nicodemus must believe in the One who was addressing him.

An Urgency to Respond

In this midnight encounter, Jesus stressed Nicodemus's urgent need to respond by faith in Him as the Son of Man. It was not enough that Nicodemus had merely heard the truth about the new birth Jesus had delivered to him. Nicodemus was pressed by Jesus to entrust his life to Him. God's sovereign activity would be to regenerate Nicodemus's heart. But Nicodemus's responsibility was that he must believe in Jesus. Here, the Lord presents to this respected figure what must occur in his life if he would enter the kingdom of heaven.

Jesus urged Nicodemus that he must take the critical step to believe in Him and exercise his will to submit his life to Him. He must place his soul into the strong hands of Him who alone can save. To do so, Nicodemus must recognize that Jesus was far more than a mere teacher like he himself was. He must see that Jesus was the Son of Man, come to rescue those perishing in their sins. The hour was late. It was urgent that Nicodemus respond.

The Serpent in the Wilderness

As Jesus called Nicodemus to believe, He provided a striking example from an Old Testament narrative, an account with which Nicodemus was undoubtedly familiar. He stated, "As Moses lifted up the serpent in the wilderness, even so must the

Son of Man be lifted up; so that whoever believes will in Him have eternal life" (vv. 14–15). Jesus intended to use this dramatic scene from Israel's wilderness wanderings with striking evangelistic force in Nicodemus's heart. The incident is found in the book of Numbers.

> The people spoke against God and Moses, "Why have you brought us up out of Egypt to die in the wilderness? For there is no food and no water, and we loathe this miserable food."
>
> The LORD sent fiery serpents among the people and they bit the people, so that many people of Israel died. So the people came to Moses and said, "We have sinned, because we have spoken against the LORD and you; intercede with the LORD, that He may remove the serpents from us." And Moses interceded for the people. Then the LORD said to Moses, "Make a fiery serpent, and set it on a standard; and it shall come about, that everyone who is bitten, when he looks at it, he will live." And Moses made a bronze serpent and set it on the standard; and it came about, that if a serpent bit any man, when he looked to the bronze serpent, he lived. (Num. 21:5–9)

Dying in Unbelief

In this riveting scene, Israel found itself in the midst of its prolonged wanderings en route to the promised land. A journey that should have taken mere weeks and months took forty years. The reason for this lengthy trip was the blatant unbelief of the people. Despite God's repeated deliverances, the Israelites continued to complain against Him and harden their hearts. They adamantly refused to trust and obey God. Consequently, God sent a devastating judgment upon His rebellious people. He caused venomous snakes to swarm through the camp and bite the people, injecting their lethal poison into them. The disobedient people began dying in the wilderness without any hope of remedy.

The people begged their leader, Moses, to pray for their recovery. Moses interceded with God, and He answered with this saving antidote. He told Moses to make a bronze serpent and lift it up on a pole. If those who were dying from the deadly venom would look at the bronze serpent, they would be healed. Admittedly, this cure seemed foolish to the natural mind. But those who chose to believe the word of God looked to the bronze snake. Those who obeyed by faith were healed, and they lived. Those who did not believe perished from the poisonous venom flowing through their veins.

Looking by Faith

The use of this wilderness incident was designed to illustrate the gospel message to Nicodemus. It urged Nicodemus to look to Jesus with the eye of faith. The bronze serpent is a "type" of Jesus, or a symbol in the Old Testament that represented Him. Throughout the Bible, there are many types that foreshadow a future reality. For example, the Passover and its spotless lamb is a type of Christ being the sinless Lamb of God, slain for the sins of the people (Exod. 12:1–13, 23–28).

Like the bronze serpent, Jesus would be lifted up on the cross to die as the substitute for those who believe in Him. The pole represented the wood cross upon which Jesus would be crucified to die. This looking to the bronze serpent is an illustration of saving faith. Believing in Jesus is like looking to Him by faith for salvation.

Jesus stressed to Nicodemus the necessity of His saving death. He emphasized, "As Moses lifted up the serpent in the wilderness, even so must the Son of Man be lifted up" (John 3:14). The word "must" underscores that Jesus *had* to die to save lost sinners. The Son of Man must die as the sin-bearing sacrifice, as He became sin for His people upon the cross. Jesus must bear the curse of the law, the penalty being eternal death. Jesus must die so that those who look to Him by faith would be healed of the deadly curse of sin. Those who look to Him will live forever.

The Necessity of Faith

In this intense exchange, Jesus stressed the necessity of faith in Himself. Jesus maintained that "whoever believes will in Him have eternal life" (v. 15). The word "believes" (*pisteuō*) means "to place confidence in someone or something." It means for a person to commit his or her life to someone or something. In this case, the object of saving faith is Jesus Christ. Nicodemus must entrust his life to Jesus Christ. He must look away from his dead religion and look exclusively to Christ.

There are many other analogies used in the Gospel of John for saving faith. This decisive act is represented as *receiving* Jesus into our life, as we would welcome guests into our homes to warmly fellowship with them (1:12). Saving faith is *obeying* Jesus, as we would heed the authoritative command from a superior in rank (3:36). It is like *eating* Jesus, as we would take bread and consume it for nourishment (6:35, 51, 53, 54, 56–68). Saving faith is like *drinking* Jesus, as we would drink water to sustain and replenish life (4:14; 7:37–38). It is *following* Jesus, as we would pursue a master teacher and place our life under the authority of his or her teaching (8:12). Saving faith is *following* Jesus, as a sheep would come after its shepherd (10:4, 27). Other such passages could be cited, but these are sufficient to give a proper picture of what it is to believe in Jesus Christ.

The Gift of Eternal Life

Jesus further explained to Nicodemus that this promised life is "eternal" (*aiōnios*), which literally means, "the life of the ages." This refers to spending future ages with God in glory. It speaks first to the quality of life that one receives in the new birth. Eternal life is the life of God in heaven come into the soul that is born again. In reality, eternal life is the life of God Himself residing in the previously empty and dead soul of a person.

This "life of the ages" is experienced now, while living in this present world. This heaven-like life begins in the present for those who are born again. Long before believers go to heaven, God has already come to live inside of them. Salvation is not merely in the future. Eternal life begins the moment we are born again and believe in Jesus Christ. The Lord will later say, "Truly, truly, I say to you, he who hears My word, and believes Him who sent Me, has eternal life, and does not come into judgment, but has passed out of death into life" (5:24). The present tense—"*has* eternal life"—stresses that this divinely given life begins the moment we believe in Jesus Christ.

Eternal life is receiving the very life of Jesus Christ Himself (1:4). Jesus claimed that He is "the bread of life" (6:35). That is, He alone gives supernatural life to those who feed upon Him. He is "living bread" (v. 51), meaning He is alive, being full of life. He alone gives life "abundantly" to those who believe in Him (10:10). This is why Jesus said that He is "the life" (11:25; 14:6). This life is found in submitting one's life to Jesus Christ in a saving relationship (17:3).

On the other hand, those without Christ have a mere empty existence, no spiritual life. This life of God is found exclusively "in Him." He is the sole source of eternal life. We cannot experience eternal life outside of knowing Jesus Christ. Apart from Him, we will experience only spiritual death. Nicodemus needed to learn this, because though he had religion, he had no eternal life.

A Never-Ending Life with God

In addition, "eternal life" speaks of the duration of this life. This present life from God will never come to an end. The relationship will never be annulled. It will continue forever, throughout all the ages to come. Once we are alive in Christ, we will always be alive in Him. Eternal life is an unbroken fellowship with God. It is a quality of life in which one's soul is fully content in Him.

Elsewhere, Jesus said, "Whoever drinks of the water that I will give him shall never thirst" (4:14). In other words, this living water will forever be fulfilling. We need look nowhere else for our souls to be satiated. After taking one sip of this divine grace, we will never thirst again. That is the unending experience of eternal life in Christ. Jesus also said, "He who believes in Me will never thirst" (6:35). Those who believe in Christ will be always fulfilled in Him. We will never have to look elsewhere to be made content. He further stated, "He who eats this bread will live forever" (v. 58). In other words, those who eat and drink of Christ will feast upon Him with pleasure forever. Jesus brings an internal gratification unlike anything this world has to offer. As we believe in Christ, we will forever have full contentment with Him.

An Everlasting Pardon and Freedom

Moreover, Jesus said, "Truly, truly, I say to you, he who hears My word, and believes Him who sent Me, has eternal life, and does not come into judgment, but has passed out of death into life" (5:24). Eternal life means the life God gives will never end. God bestows a pardon that is irrevocable. If a believer could be pardoned for five years and then lose his or her salvation, it would not be eternal life. Instead, it would be merely five-year life. If a person could be saved for ten years and then lose his or her salvation, it would be only ten-year life. But God has given *eternal* life to those who believe. This is a life that will never end. It is eternal because it lasts through all eternity.

Jesus would further state, "Truly, truly, I say to you, everyone who commits sin is the slave of sin. The slave does not remain in the house forever; the son does remain forever. So if the Son makes you free, you will be free indeed" (8:34–36). When we are born again, God delivers us from the domination of sin. Without Christ, every person is under the wrath of God (3:36). All have sinned, and the wages of sin is death (Rom. 3:23; 6:23). Since God is holy and just, He must punish the rebellious sinner. To believe in Christ includes turning from a lifestyle of sin and turning to Christ with a submissive heart. To believe is to enter into salvation from the wrath of God.

When we are regenerated, we are immediately transferred from the kingdom of darkness into the kingdom of God. This dramatic deliverance occurs when the Holy Spirit gives the second birth from above. This miracle gives new power to live in obedience to the word of God. Those who are born again no longer follow worldly desires. Instead, we who believe are freed from the stronghold that sin once had on our life. Jesus said, "If the Son makes you free, you will be free indeed" (John 8:36). The one delivered will *never* return to the tyranny of his or her old master to live in bondage to sin. Eternal life in Christ means forever being freed from slavery. The soul's new master is Christ.

Living Forever with God

For example, when Jesus received the report about Lazarus's death, He traveled to Bethany, where Lazarus had lived. Jesus was approached by Martha, one of Lazarus's sisters, who stated, "Lord, if You had been here, my brother would not have died" (11:21). With this bold assertion, Jesus responded, "I am the resurrection and the life; he who believes in Me will live even if he dies, and everyone who lives and believes in Me will never die. Do you believe this?" (vv. 25–26). Those who are made alive in the new birth will never die spiritually.

Every believer who physically dies will spiritually live forever with God. After death, those who are born again will pass immediately into the presence of God. Resurrection life extends far beyond the grave. No one who is born again will ever be condemned and sentenced to hell. This debt incurred by sin was paid in full by Christ for all who believe in Him. God will never require payment for that sin again. Once we are made alive in Christ, we are forever alive in Him. Those who are born again and believe in Jesus will truly live forever with God.

The Spirit Forever with Us

And when we believe, the Spirit forever lives with us. When Jesus gathered His disciples into the upper room, He promised that after His departure, He would send the Holy Spirit to be with them permanently. "I will ask the Father, and He will give you another Helper, that He may be with you forever" (John 14:16). This other "Helper" is the Holy Spirit. As the Paraclete, He indwells all disciples "forever." Through the new birth, every believer possesses the Holy Spirit now and forever. No believer will ever forfeit the residing presence of the Spirit. No life indwelt by this divine Helper will ever be vacated by Him.

Each of the previous verses teaches the permanent nature of eternal life. Those who are born again possess eternal life. This life does not begin once we step into eternity after death. Instead, eternal life starts the moment we are born again. Possessing eternal life is always represented in the present tense. Eternal life is the immediate possession of all who are birthed from above. Whoever believes in the Son is instantly given eternal life. All believers have unending life that can never be forfeited.

To forever live an eternal quality of life brings abundant joy. Every believer can be comforted that we are eternally pardoned from all sins and forever released from the slavery to sin to which we once were bound. We are forever living in reality with God, and forever having His Spirit indwell and empower all who trust in Jesus Christ. All of these promises are unconditional and unending.

Never Born Again, Again

The miracle of regeneration is a one-time act. It will never be revoked and then repeated. A person is born again once for all time. This initial work of saving grace is permanent and endures throughout the ages to come. No one is ever born again, again. The divine act of regeneration can never be reversed, never revoked. Being born again can never be negated, never made null and void. It is the eternal life of the ever-living God that lives within believers for all time.

You Must Be Born Again

First, no matter how religious you may be, you must be born again in order to enter the kingdom of heaven. The same is true no matter how irreligious you may be. You can have all the religious knowledge in the world, but you must still be born from above. A full head can still have an empty heart. God must work in your heart in order for you to enter His kingdom.

Second, you must rely completely on your personal faith in Jesus Christ to deliver you from eternal punishment. If you will commit yourself to Christ, He will rescue you from the wages of your sin. If you do not, you will be the object of His eternal punishment forever, as the due penalty of your sin.

Third, you must walk in obedience to His commands, not in order to be born again but *because* you are. What He has done in your life should cause you to give Him glory and praise for the rest of your life. This is the validating proof of being born again—this fruit of righteousness from the new life God gives you.

What encouragement this is for all believers! We are just as surely destined for heaven as though we have already been there ten thousand years. May you rest in the eternal security of His saving grace—the greatest comfort for every believing soul.

fifteen

Rescuing Love

For God so loved the world, that He gave His only begotten Son, that whoever believes in Him shall not perish, but have eternal life. For God did not send the Son into the world to judge the world, but that the world might be saved through Him.

JOHN 3:16–17

The driving force within the heart of God that sent Jesus Christ into this world was His great love for those perishing in their sins. Rather than destroy this sinful world in His wrath, God chose instead to crush His Son upon the cross with the righteous anger we deserved. This amazing love of God for those without hope in this world lies at the heart of the new birth.

The love of God for sinners is the crown jewel that sparkles most brightly atop the glittering diadem of the gospel. Here in the love of the Father for sinners is the priceless treasure that exceeds all other precious stones in its incomparable value. If we were forced to select only one verse to describe the great love of God for those outside His kingdom, it would be John 3:16, which has to be the most beloved text in the entire Bible.

What makes this text so valuable is that it was spoken by the greatest Teacher who ever walked this earth—Jesus Christ. It identifies the greatest Lover in the universe—God the Father. It describes the greatest sacrifice ever made—God gave His only Son to die for sinners. It promises the greatest rescue of those who believe—they will not perish. It extends the greatest offer to whoever will believe in Jesus Christ—eternal life. We can easily understand the great appeal this verse has had throughout the centuries.

In this one monumental statement, the heart of the gospel was made known to Nicodemus. Here, Jesus announced the good news of salvation to this highly respected individual who stood outside the kingdom. It is the message of the love of God in reconciling sinners to Himself through His Son, Jesus Christ. Nicodemus must exercise faith in Christ to receive eternal life. Nothing that Jesus would say to him could rise to a higher level than this central truth. It is the loftiest pinnacle of the message of salvation.

Let us look carefully at this golden text of Scripture that has captivated lives down through the last two millennia.

A Continuation of Thought

This deeply loved verse begins with the small word "For." This little conjunction indicates that this verse is a continuation of thought from the statement Jesus made in the previous verse.

In other words, this verse is inseparably connected to the preceding text and serves to advance this unfolding narrative and building argument. The necessity of believing in Jesus Christ and receiving eternal life, as stated in verse 15, is further developed in verse 16.

God Is Love

Jesus states that God the Father sent Him into this world to rescue perishing sinners. Here is Jesus's own commentary, succinctly stated, on His mission in this world. Everything in God's plan of salvation flows from His own loving heart. The Father loved His chosen ones before the world began. He authored the gospel and gave His chosen ones to His Son to be His chosen bride. The Father then determined to send the Son into the world to die for those given to Him. Further, it was the Father along with the Son who sent the Holy Spirit into the world to cause their new birth and usher them into His kingdom.

It was the love of God the Father that initiated this saving mission. The Bible states, "God is love" (1 John 4:8, 16). This means it is the very nature of God to love. His love is unconditional, not based upon the merit of the one loved. The love of God rises from within Himself because He chooses to love, and is so great. He chooses to love the unlovely.

God has chosen to set His love on those who do not deserve it. God has not loved the world because it is lovable. This world is vile and offensive to His holiness. This world has rebelled against Him and provoked His righteous anger. God is full of indignation every day toward the wicked. Yet God has chosen to love those upon whom His fierce wrath rests. This is what makes God's love so amazing. He loves those who are unholy in His sight, which is all of us. He demonstrates love toward His enemies. He loves because He is love.

A Comprehensive Love

God has loved sinners from eternity past, before He ever created them. This eternal nature of God's love for this world is indicated by the tense of the verb "loved." The love of God reaches back to eternity past. That is when He first loved those He chose to save. It was then that He foreknew His elect (Rom. 8:29). The word "foreknew" (*proginōskō*) means He previously loved His own with a distinguishing love. The apostle Paul writes, "In love He predestined us to adoption as sons" (Eph. 1:4–5). This is to say, before time began, God loved His chosen ones. God loved those who belong to Him long before He made them. He loved them before they ever sinned.

The eternal love of God the Father came to full realization within time when He sent His Son into the world. His love for His chosen ones came to its greatest demonstration at Calvary, when God delivered over His Son to death on their behalf (Rom. 8:32). This love of the Father extends throughout human history in the free offer of the gospel. Moreover, the love of the Father is still active as He cares and provides for His sons and daughters. This love will never wane. It will continue throughout eternity future, when He will bring every believer into His presence forever.

Love from Above

The apostle John reinforced this truth when he wrote, "See how great a love the Father has bestowed on us, that we would be called children of God" (1 John 3:1). Specifically, we must carefully consider the nature of this divine love. It is described as "how great" (*potapos*), which literally means a love that is "of another country." In other words, the love of God has come down from another world. It is an out-of-this-world love, unlike any love this world has ever seen.

This divine love is far higher than any love that originates in this world. It is a love of another realm that belongs exclusively to God. The love of God far exceeds any love that has been demonstrated by humankind. The love of a husband for his wife or the love of a mother for her children does not compare to the love of God for His chosen ones. There is nothing with which to compare His love.

The Vastness and Greatness of His Love

As this verse continues, Jesus adds that God so loved "the world" (v. 16). The term "world" (*kosmos*) refers to fallen humanity that is defiled by sin. It describes the general realm of the sinful human race that is condemned and under divine wrath. And it refers to the whole human race, both Jews and gentiles, which is comprised of "Greeks and . . . barbarians" (Rom. 1:14). Despite their religious or social standing, God loves both the wise and the foolish, the religious and irreligious of this world.

So vast is the scope of God's love that it reaches out to include those "from every tribe and tongue and people and nation" (Rev. 5:9). Every "tribe" includes every ethnic group in the world, from Southeast Asians to Northern Canadians. Every "tongue" includes every language group, from Russian to Spanish to Gaelic. Every "people" refers to every racial group, whether in Scandinavia or West Africa or Australia. Every "nation" identifies people from every political group, whether in an Eastern European country or small South Pacific island.

The nature of God's love for the world is not simply a matter of His feelings. It is not a mushy or sentimental love. God loved by choosing to sacrifice His Son to die for wretched sinners. It is the very nature of God's love to sacrificially give to rescue those under His wrath.

The greatness of God's love is seen in the fact "that He gave His only begotten Son" (John 3:16) to die in the place of all who would put their trust in Him. True love does not seek to take from others but rather gives to them. In fact, authentic love sacrificially gives of itself to seek the highest good for the one loved. Genuine love is costly and expensive. True love comes at a great price by the One who loves. This is how God has loved this world, by making the highest priced sacrifice. He loved by giving His Son to die upon the cross.

In loving the world, God gave the costliest gift ever given by sacrificing His "only begotten Son." "Only begotten" (*monogenēs*) means "one of a kind, unique, the only one of its kind." In other words, Jesus is the only Son of God, not one of many. "Only begotten" means that Jesus is a Son like no other son who has existed. He is in a class by Himself. This fact that Jesus is God's *only* Son exponentially heightens the demonstration of the Father's love.

Concerning this sacrificial love, the apostle Paul writes, "God demonstrates His own love toward us, in that while we were yet sinners, Christ died for us" (Rom. 5:8). This kind of selfless, undeserved love is what God so vividly displayed at the cross. The apostle John adds, "By this the love of God was manifested in us, that God has sent His only begotten Son into the world so that we might live through Him. In this is love, not that we loved God, but that He loved us and sent His Son to be the propitiation for our sins" (1 John 4:9–10). The greatness of God's love is evidenced by the greatness of His sacrifice.

Responding to This Love

In his pronouncement to Nicodemus, Jesus further states that those who are perishing must receive this love. The only right response to such love is to believe in Him. For Nicodemus to believe in Jesus Christ means more than the mere intellectual acknowledgment of what Jesus was saying. It involves more than Nicodemus having warm feelings or sentimental emotions toward Jesus. Saving faith runs much deeper. It would require of him much more. The love of God demanded the commitment of Nicodemus's life to Jesus Christ. It required that he fully trust Him as Lord and Savior.

The word "whoever" indicates that this was a free offer being extended to Nicodemus—but he must receive it. Despite his past sins, this gospel and this love were being offered to him.

A Love That Rescues—Forever

Further, Jesus tells Nicodemus *why* he must believe in Him. It is imperative so that he will "not perish" (v. 16). The clear implication is that Nicodemus was at that very moment perishing. Apart from the new birth, the just punishment of God upon his sin would eternally destroy his soul. The word "perish" (*apollymi*) means "to be destroyed." Nicodemus was dying in his sin. Though he looked respectable on the outside, he was dead on the inside. He was headed to eternal destruction, where he would suffer forever.

This message for Nicodemus was urgent. Unless he would be born again and believe in Jesus Christ, eternal destruction awaited him in a real place called hell. However, if he would act now and entrust his life to Christ, he would not perish but be rescued from eternal ruin. This step of faith was necessary for him to be delivered from eternal destruction in the lake of fire and brimstone. If he would turn away from his self-righteousness and embrace Jesus, Jesus would save Nicodemus from the divine wrath that was already abiding over his life (John 3:36).

There is one final aspect of this divine love that Nicodemus must hear. Jesus promised that if he would believe in Him, he would "have eternal life" (v. 16). Eternal life *is* knowing God in a personal way. Jesus later prayed, "This is eternal life, that they may know You, the only true God, and Jesus Christ whom You have sent" (17:3). This is the promise extended to Nicodemus. Though he was separated from God by his sins, he may enter into the personal knowledge of God through faith in Christ.

The Reason for the Mission

Jesus then provides a reinforced explanation for His coming into the world. He states, "For God did not send the Son into the world to judge the world, but that the world might be saved through Him" (3:17). Jesus explained this truth with a negative denial followed by a positive assertion. The Lord begins with why He did *not* come into this world. There is no room for misunderstanding as Jesus speaks about His coming. "For God did not send the Son into the world to judge the world" (v. 17). The primary purpose of His coming was not to carry out a mission of judgment. Though everyone who does not believe in Jesus is condemned (vv. 18–19), God's intent in sending His Son was for their salvation, not their condemnation. Sinners were already under divine judgment because of their sin. There would be no purpose in sending the Son to judge sinners, because they were already in a state of condemnation before God.

The verb "judge" (*krinō*) literally means "to distinguish, to separate." The idea is of selecting one thing above another. Therefore, the meaning is God's divine differentiation in His dealings with people. To be judged is the very opposite of what it means to be saved from God's wrath. It means the execution of divine wrath upon the sinner.

In the church, it can be easy to see Christ as a judging Savior. Granted, He will return a second time to judge the world. But His primary purpose in coming was not to judge. Instead, His mission was motivated by the *love* of the Father. His goal was to reconcile humankind to God. When we proclaim Christ crucified, it is a stumbling block to those who do not know Him. But to the redeemed, it is the pinnacle of triumph. The good news is a cause for joy to those who believe.

Jesus then states the positive reason for His coming into the world: He was sent by God "that the world might be saved through Him" (v. 17). The word "saved" (*sōzō*) means "a deliverance from destruction, a rescue from ruin." This was clearly His chief purpose in coming into this world. It was to intervene amid the threatening situation in which the human race found itself. Jesus came in order to save sinners from eternal punishment.

This stated purpose was clear. At His birth, the angel announced to Joseph, "You shall call His name Jesus, for He will save His people from their sins" (Matt. 1:21). The name Jesus, which means "the Lord saves," reveals His purpose of entrance into the human race. Jesus explained, "It is not those who are healthy who need a physician, but those who are sick" (Matt. 9:12). He came to heal the souls of those who were dying in their sins.

Jesus announces the purpose of His mission in the account of the conversion of Zacchaeus. He states, "For the Son of Man has come to seek and to save that which was lost" (Luke 19:10). He came to rescue the lost from eternal harm to their soul. He came to deliver them from the threatening danger of God's impending judgment. Sin has placed humankind on a path headed for eternal damnation. But God sent Christ to save those facing divine wrath.

Despite what Nicodemus thought about himself, he needed to be rescued from perishing in the eternal flames of hell. He needed to be delivered from the already-kindled, righteous anger of God against him (John 3:36). This is the peril in which Nicodemus found himself in that moment. He stood in dire need of being delivered from the wrath to come.

Sent by the Father

Jesus did not undertake this mission of salvation on His own initiative. He was not self-willed in deciding to come into this world. Being lifted up on the cross in order to redeem those who would believe in Him was the eternal purpose of God the Father. Jesus stressed that it was God who "[sent] the Son into the world" (v. 17). In other words, it was the will of the Father to send the Son to rescue the lost who were perishing. By the greatness of the love of God, He sent His only begotten Son to redeem those who were the objects of His wrath.

This sending of Jesus by the Father is a major emphasis made throughout the Gospel of John. It was God the Father who sent

God the Son (3:34); God sent Christ to speak the words of God (5:36, 38). God the Father gave Jesus works to accomplish to testify to His deity (6:29, 38, 57). Jesus was sent by the Father to do His will (7:29). Jesus knows the Father who sent Him (8:42). Jesus came from the Father, because the Father sent Him (10:36). Jesus is the Son of God, sent into the world by the Father (11:42). Jesus affirms He accomplished the work the Father gave Him to do (17:3, 8, 18, 21, 23, 25). Jesus comforts His followers with peace, reminding them that as the Father sent Him into the world, so He sends them into the world (20:21).

If Nicodemus should reject the offer of salvation being extended to him by Jesus, he would be rejecting God Himself, who sent Jesus to testify to the truth. It is impossible to be right with God while rejecting the One whom He sent, the Lord Jesus Christ. The Father and the Son are one in their saving purpose (10:30).

Standing at the Crossroads

At this very moment, Nicodemus found himself standing at the turning point of his life. He had been traveling the broad path headed for destruction. He must choose to travel a new path, the road headed toward life. In order to do so, he must exit the broad road that accommodates his dead religion. He must enter by faith the narrow path prepared and paved by the Father. He must leave the crowded path traveled by many and choose the isolated path traveled by few. This is the decisive step of faith that Nicodemus must take. It would be the most important decision he could ever make.

If you are born again, can you remember standing at this same intersection of your life? Can you recollect being confronted with this same choice? Do you recall how you had been travel-ing the broad path?

The Time Is Now

I have witnessed many people being born again by God's grace. Many, in the eyes of others, would have been considered the least likely to be saved. Most were like Nicodemus, who had all the outward indications of spiritual status but was devoid of the inward reality. It may be that you are presently standing where Nicodemus once stood. Perhaps you have not yet believed in Jesus Christ. If that is true, this is an important moment for you.

This is a time when the Spirit of God can work in your soul. Perhaps He has convicted you that you are on the wrong path, headed in the wrong direction. If this is where you find yourself, seek the Lord while He may be found. Call upon Him while He is near. I urge you to commit your life to Jesus. He is the Son of God, the One sent by the Father into this world to save perishing sinners. Turn your heart to Him. Believe in Him, and you will be saved.

sixteen

Divided World

He who believes in Him is not judged; he who does not
believe has been judged already, because he has not
believed in the name of the only begotten Son of God.
This is the judgment, that the Light has come into the
world, and men loved the darkness rather than the Light,
for their deeds were evil. For everyone who does evil
hates the Light, and does not come to the Light for fear
that his deeds will be exposed. But he who practices
the truth comes to the Light, so that his deeds may be
manifested as having been wrought in God.

JOHN 3:18–21

In the mind of God, there are only two groups in the world into which everyone finds themselves. By His estimate, there are not three or four groups into which humankind is divided. Neither are there five or ten groups. As God sees this world, there are only two distinct groups. These two classifications are polar opposites, as radically different as they can be.

We are all sharply divided between those who believe in Jesus Christ and those who do not. To put it another way, there are those who are not judged by God and those who are judged by Him. There are those who love the Light, Jesus Christ, and those who hate Him. There are those who come out of spiritual darkness and those who desire to remain in it. There are those who live the truth and those who practice evil.

There are many other ways to classify these two groups of people. But the fact remains that there are only these two groups in the world. As defined by Jesus, there are those born of the Spirit and those born of the flesh, who remain in their carnal state. There are those who are saved by the Savior and those who are perishing in their sins. There are those who are spiritually alive and those who are spiritually dead. There are no other categories in which we can find ourselves.

This sharp distinction is reinforced by Jesus as He brings His dialogue with Nicodemus to its conclusion. The Lord made this a black-and-white matter. There are no shades of gray when it comes to who is in the kingdom of God and who is not. Either Nicodemus was a citizen of the heavenly kingdom or he was an alien to it. He could only find himself in one of these two categories and no other.

In no uncertain terms, Jesus has pointedly clarified that Nicodemus was currently outside the kingdom of God. This was startling and unsettling for Nicodemus to hear, because he had never seen himself in this divine light. To this point, he had been deceived about where he stands with God. It never dawned on him that he was a spiritual corpse in need of eternal life. He had not been aware that he needed to be born again. Until now.

To drive this home, Jesus draws a sharp line of distinction between these two groups of people. As their dialogue concludes, Jesus makes three clarifying distinctions, which serve to bring Nicodemus to the place of a deep awareness of his need for regeneration. The purpose was that he would put his trust in Jesus, the only Savior of sinners.

Not Judged or Judged?

The first contrast Jesus makes is between those who are presently not judged by God and those who are judged. The Lord makes this distinction crystal clear. "He who believes in Him is not judged; he who does not believe has been judged already" (John 3:18). By this statement, Nicodemus must conclude whether he is or is not being judged by God. Jesus clarified that if he believes in Him, he is not judged. But if he does not believe in Him, he is judged already.

At this moment, Nicodemus learned he is *already* judged by God. There was nothing he needed to do to become condemned before God. He was already found guilty because of his sin. God is the Judge in the Supreme Court of heaven. Nicodemus was presently under the death sentence as pronounced by Jesus. All that mattered was not how Nicodemus appeared before people but how he stood before God. This highly respected ruler has been weighed in God's balances and been found wanting.

Already Condemned

The formal execution of this sentence awaits the last day. Nevertheless, the outcome of this final judgment is certain, as it presently stands. Nicodemus was already condemned before God because Adam's sin was credited to every member of humanity (Rom. 5:12–21). This includes Nicodemus. What is more, his own sins condemn him before God (3:23; 6:23). But ultimately he was condemned because he had not believed in Jesus Christ. The high court of heaven judges all unbelievers, long before the final judgment. At that very moment, this was where Nicodemus found himself.

If you realize you stand condemned in the court of heaven, cry out to God, who is merciful to those who believe in His Son. He will extend grace to you if you will humble yourself before Him. Reflect on where you stand with God. Run to Christ, who is the Savior for sinners.

Committing Cosmic Treason

To further secure Nicodemus's attention, Jesus emphasized the serious nature of his unbelief. The Lord explained that judgment has come "because he has not believed in the name of the only begotten Son of God" (John 3:18). According to this statement, the object of saving faith must be the name of Jesus Christ. "Name" refers to all that Jesus is in His person and mission. If he is to enter the kingdom, Nicodemus must believe that Jesus is more than a teacher come from God and more than a miracle worker. He must believe that Jesus is who He claimed to be as the Son of God (vv. 16, 17, 18) who was sent by God (v. 14) from heaven (v. 13) in order to be lifted up to die (v. 14). He must believe that Jesus alone can rescue him from the judgment of God.

The seriousness of unbelief is that it rejects God by refusing to believe in His Son, Jesus Christ. Unbelief toward Jesus defiantly repudiates God's plan of salvation. It dishonors God by disregarding His only Son. It brazenly calls Jesus Christ a liar, who says that the gospel is true. It utterly rejects that Jesus is "the only begotten Son of God" (v. 18). Unbelief denounces Jesus as merely one more human teacher who is unfit to be trusted. Is it any wonder that an unbeliever like Nicodemus was judged already? He participated, as all unbelievers do, in high treason against God.

Light or Darkness?

The second contrast Jesus makes between the two groups in humanity is between the Light and the darkness. The Lord pronounced, "This is the judgment, that the Light has come into the world, and men loved the darkness rather than the Light, for their deeds were evil" (v. 19). By these words, Jesus represented Himself as "the Light" who has come into this world of spiritual darkness.

This is not a new distinction, because He has been already described by John as light (1:4–5, 9). Jesus will later describe Himself again as "the Light of the world" (8:12; 9:5; 12:35). As the Light, Jesus has come to reveal the Father to this sin-darkened world. By this same metaphor, Jesus also represents Himself as being perfectly holy in His character. Like a blazing light, He has come to expose the evil deeds of humanity.

However, rather than coming to the Light to have his sins revealed and, thus, seek God's grace, like all humanity Nicodemus had a natural aversion to the Light. He loved the darkness because it hid his sins. He hated the Light because it revealed his deeds as being evil. He willfully rejected the truth in order to keep his sins hidden. He could continue to pretend his sins did not exist, but this would not deny their reality.

The coming of the Light has brought judgment upon the world. In this context, the term "judgment" (*krisis*) means a divine verdict rendered upon humanity's sins. Jesus was sent into the world for the primary purpose of salvation, but the inevitable result of rejecting the truth is His coming judgment. No one is in a neutral state before God, not even Nicodemus. Either he believes in Him and is not judged or he remains in the darkness and is judged by Him.

Have you ever found yourself hiding from God? Withdrawing from the truth? How did Jesus rescue you? Did His gracious light shine on you and expose your wrongs?

Truth or Evil?

In the third contrast, Jesus makes the clear distinction between truth and evil. He explains, "For everyone who does evil hates the Light, and does not come to the Light for fear that his deeds will be exposed. But he who practices the truth comes to the Light, so that his deeds may be manifested as having been wrought in God" (John 3:20–21). Jesus is saying that the total antithesis of the truth of God is the committing of evil deeds. In other words, the rejection of the truth inevitably leads to the practice of sinful deeds.

In no uncertain terms, Jesus announces, "For everyone who does evil hates the Light" (v. 20). Unbelievers actually hate the Light. It is not that they have some small love for it, or are merely neutral toward it. Instead, they utterly despise the Light. They love their sin but hate Christ, the Light of the world. To hate the Light is to reject Him. Moreover, it is to refuse the necessity of the new birth.

Jesus stressed that the one who hates the Light "does not come to the Light for fear that his deeds will be exposed"

(v. 20). More sad than a child afraid of the dark is an adult afraid of the Light. The word "exposed" (*elenchthē*) means a manifestation of evil in a person's life with the conviction and shame that come with it. Consequently, the unbeliever who refuses to come to Christ does so to avoid dealing with the sin in his or her life. This is exactly where Nicodemus found himself.

Keeping a Safe Distance

As a pastor, I have known many people like Nicodemus. They linger in the shadows in order to avoid the Light. They want to live for the world yet have heaven at the same time. In their unbelief, they want to keep Christ at arm's length—at a safe distance. They want what He offers without having to deal with His demands.

In the last church I pastored, I had a particular section in the worship center of the church where certain women came to church without their unbelieving husbands. They would sit together and encourage each other while living with their unconverted husbands. The men to whom they were married came to church on Christmas and Easter. Rarely would they make more than this token appearance to appease their wives. They would sit in church with unseen "do not disturb" signs hanging around their necks. They were terrified of the truth they would hear as the word was preached.

Coming to the Light

On the other hand, Jesus taught that a true believer lives in a completely different realm. Rather than avoiding the Light, the one who is born again comes to the Light. Jesus asserts, "But he who practices the truth comes to the Light, so that his deeds may be manifested as having been wrought in God" (v. 21). Those who come to the Light will live in the light. Having believed in Jesus Christ, we will "practice the truth." The Light will have exposed the sin in our life, leading us to repent of our sin and turn away from its pursuit. This is what it means to come to the Light.

For believers, the Light leads us down the narrow path. The Light points to the way of holiness in the darkness of this world. This walk of personal purity will not consist of only a few momentary steps. Each person who comes to the Light "practices the truth" (v. 21). This refers to an ongoing lifestyle, a long-term pursuit of following the truth.

Having saving faith in Christ means that our "deeds may be manifested as having been wrought in God" (v. 21). Because of the regeneration, believers will live differently than we formerly did when we lived in darkness. The Spirit works in each new life, giving us new power to conduct ourselves in a manner pleasing to God. By being born again, believers will live holy lives by the governing principle of our new nature.

A Time for Decision

At last, this memorable encounter between Nicodemus and Jesus concludes. How would Nicodemus respond? Would he come to the Light and believe in Jesus Christ, beginning a new path? Or would he remain in the darkness and continue practicing evil deeds?

Nicodemus must respond without delay. Now that the truth of the gospel has been made known to him, he must not hesitate to answer the call to decide. Nicodemus must answer this summons issued by the Lord Jesus Christ. It is not enough that he has heard the gospel truth. He must now answer this divine message.

But there is no response from Nicodemus recorded in this narrative. Perhaps this Bible teacher needed more time to process what he had heard. This truth that he heard from Jesus completely caught him off guard. He was stunned by this abrupt message from Christ and thrown back on his heels. And we do not know what, if anything, he said.

Many times, I have shared the gospel with someone, and they would not respond by committing their life to Christ. Sometimes it is because they are not yet convinced of the truthfulness of Scripture. At other times it is because they are not ready to forsake their lifestyle of sin. Or it is because they are concerned with what others will think. Though this rejection of Christ has saddened my heart, I had to be willing to surrender their soul to God rather than manipulate a response.

That is exactly what we see Jesus doing here. He understood that Nicodemus was not yet ready to confess his sin and believe the gospel message. At this point, Jesus was content to sow the good seed. He would wait for the harvest of Nicodemus's soul that would come later.

Two Years Later

The next time that we hear from Nicodemus is approximately two years later. This initial encounter occurred in the first year of Jesus's public ministry. Nicodemus will later reappear in the Gospel of John during the third year of Jesus's public ministry, during a time of increasing controversy surrounding Jesus. The people were divided in their opinion regarding who He was, eventually leading to His crucifixion.

In this heated moment, the religious leaders of Israel tried to have Jesus arrested. They sent officials to seize Him, but they returned empty-handed because they were awestruck by what they heard from Him. When confronted and asked why they did not bring Jesus back as they had been dispatched to do, the officials replied, "Never has a man spoken the way this man speaks" (John 7:46). That is to say, they were astonished by the penetrating force of the truth He presented.

The Pharisees then asked, "No one of the rulers or Pharisees has believed in Him, has he?" (v. 48). The truth was, there was at least one who was giving Jesus serious consideration. It was Nicodemus, who stepped forward and said, "Our Law does not judge a man unless it first hears from him and knows what he is doing, does it?" (v. 51). Though this was not an open confession of Jesus, it does indicate his desire to slow down the opposition against Him.

It can be rightly assumed that Nicodemus had seriously taken to heart what Jesus said to him two years ago. He had not discarded the truth he heard during his late-night meeting with Him. The Lord's teaching about the necessity of the new birth and saving faith found a lodging in Nicodemus's mind. The seed was planted, and it appears that now it was beginning to germinate.

Whenever anyone plants the seed of the gospel, we know its growth is not dependent upon us. Paul said, "I planted, Apollos watered, but God was causing the growth. So then neither the one who plants nor the one who waters is anything, but God who causes the growth" (1 Cor. 3:6–7). Here, Christ Himself planted the seed, and God the Father caused it to germinate in His perfect timing.

Stepping Out of the Shadows

Fast-forward to the end of Jesus's life. The Lord has been crucified as the most controversial and despised figure of His day. So provocative was Jesus that, after His arrest, even His disciples could not afford to remain identified with Him. They were hiding behind closed doors, protecting their own lives at this volatile time. Only John and several faithful women, including Jesus's mother, remained with Him until the end as He hung upon the cross. This was a dangerous time to be identified with Jesus, whom many considered to be leading a revolution to overthrow the government.

When it came time to bury the body of Jesus, though, two secret believers stepped forward to claim His corpse. Their intent was to give Him an honorable burial (John 19:38). Joseph of Arimathea asked for the body, and Pilate granted his request. Joining him in this perilous endeavor was none other than Nicodemus, undoubtedly out of sincere devotion for Christ. This heroic act certainly exposed Joseph and Nicodemus to great danger. Showing loyalty to a public enemy like Jesus of Nazareth was not safe. Nevertheless, these two men courageously stepped up, undoubtedly true believers in Jesus Christ.

It is reasonable to assume that Nicodemus has come to a firm commitment to Christ. Though this is not explicitly stated, he nevertheless shows the signs of a man who has genuinely identified himself with the Lord Jesus Christ. He gives evidence of having crossed the line to become a follower of Jesus. He demonstrates a willingness to suffer for Christ in the face of danger. He appears to have changed his allegiance from hating the Light to loving it. He turned from living in darkness to walking in the Light. He is willing to risk his life for the One who was delivered to die in order to purchase his salvation.

A Positive Ending

Nicodemus has come a long way, spiritually speaking, from his initial private meeting with Jesus. At that time, he was fearful anyone would see him meeting with Jesus, but now he is willing to risk persecution and possible martyrdom for Christ. Here is a man unashamed of Jesus before a sinful generation, willing to be identified with Jesus—whatever it may cost him.

This is what saving faith does. It owns Jesus as Lord and Savior before the eyes of a watching world. Saving faith embraces Jesus, whatever the outcome. It turns its back to the world and follows Christ, even in the face of mounting difficulty. Saving faith comes out of the darkness and steps into the Light.

The Reality of Your Life

May this experience of Nicodemus be the reality of your life. Though your personal circumstances will be entirely different, I pray that you know what it is to be born again. May you be birthed into the kingdom of God. May you believe in Jesus Christ as your Savior and Lord. Then you will have experienced the most powerful work of God anyone could ever know.

If you have not yet been born from above, I urge you to ask God to make this real in your life. This is the change of heart you need to enter the kingdom of God. You need to receive new life in Jesus Christ.

May you know what it is to be born again, to become a living miracle by the power and love of God alone.

Acknowledgments

This book is the result of many people who have collaborated their efforts to make it what it is. I want to thank:

James Lawson, my son, who urged me to put this work into print.

Rachel Webb, my administrative assistant, who tirelessly typed this entire manuscript.

Grace Anne Bills, my daughter and the ministry coordinator for OnePassion, who read every line of this book multiple times and made many helpful additions.

Carissa Arend, my editor at OnePassion, who edited this manuscript.

Brian Thomasson, executive editor for Baker Books, who saw the value in this project.

Lindsey Spoolstra, project editor for Baker Books, who oversaw the editing.

Patti Brinks, art director for Baker Books, for designing the beautiful cover.

Erin Smith, assistant marketing director for Baker Books, for strategizing the visibility of this book.

Anne Lawson, my wife, who has encouraged me throughout our marriage and my many years of ministry.

Steven J. Lawson (ThM, Dallas Theological Seminary; DMin, Reformed Theological Seminary) is president of OnePassion Ministries, a ministry designed to bring about biblical reformation in the church today by teaching and preaching the word of God and training others to do likewise. Lawson is the professor of preaching at The Master's Seminary, where he is also dean of the doctor of ministry program and serves on the board of directors. A teaching fellow and board member of Ligonier Ministries, he is also the executive editor of *Expositor* magazine. Lawson is a regular speaker at conferences such as the Shepherds' Conference and the Ligonier National Conference, and his preaching has taken him across the country and around the world. The author of twenty-nine books, Lawson lives in Dallas, Texas.

CONNECT WITH
Dr. Steven J. Lawson

OnePassionMinistries.org/drstevenjlawson

 DRSTEVENJLAWSON

Connect with
BakerBooks
Relevant. Intelligent. Engaging.

Sign up for announcements about
new and upcoming titles at

BakerBooks.com/SignUp

@ReadBakerBooks